Entertaining for Eternity
with Heavenly Hospitality

Nan McCullough

ISBN Number 1-56399-308-2

What others say....

Vonette Bright, Co-founder of Campus Crusade for Christ.
"Nan McCullough has a great heart for evangelism. Being a great hostess too, Nan combines easy 'How to's' from her vast experiences. She has served on our staff for almost four decades. You will learn how to add meaning to any event that will bring rewards throughout eternity."

Janet Huckabee, wife of Governor Mike Huckabee.
"It has been a treat for me, as a governor's wife, and for other First Ladies to experience Nan's hospitality. I've watched as Nan has guided our friends through the wonderful world of entertaining with such a gracious spirit of love. This book will guide you through that same journey to share the uniqueness of feeling special through entertaining with God's greatest creation, a friend."

Jeannie Blocher, President and founder of Body and Soul Fitness.
"Nan graciously shared her first edition of Heavenly Hospitality with the instructors of Body and Soul Fitness and we have all been encouraged by the easy and fun ways Nan has guided us to share our homes with others with a purpose in mind- sharing our faith! You, too, will be blessed by this creative approach to relationship-building with a purpose."

Mary Clement, Past President of Congressional Club.
"There is no one better than Nan McCullough when it comes to teaching the Bible through real life examples. She can have you laughing one minute and crying the next as she uses illustrations to meet you where you are in life. Her trustworthiness and encouragement endears her to you immediately."

Bobbi Lungren, wife of Congressman Dan Lungren of California.
"Nan has the wonderful ability to combine beautiful events in her home with a deeper spiritual dimension. I had the opportunity to attend one of her 'teas' and it was as well done as tea at the Plaza in New York City. Her homemade selections were even better! Her real charm, however, is her warmth and graciousness; her sharing of the love of the Lord. What a combination!"

Jane Daniel, Director of McLean Bible Church small groups at Tyson's Campus
"Nan McCullough is a gifted communicator with a pulse on the women of the New Millennium. Her skill and her education makes her an articulate speaker and her years with Campus Crusade for Christ, as a wife and mother, mentor and friend to Capital Hill wives give her something to say. Our women are always delighted when she speaks! Her Heavenly Hospitality Workshops have been a hit with the ladies at our church. Many have been motivated to open the doors of their homes in many ways. Only eternity will reveal the true impact of this type of entertaining."

Key to the symbols used in this book:

 indicates a page reference to later in the book.

 indicates a website reference you can utilize.

The verses in this book were taken primarily from the New International Version and the Amplified Bible (Zondervan), as well as the Living Bible and the New Living Translation (Tyndale House Publishers).

Entertaining for Eternity
with Heavenly Hospitality

As Christians, we wring our hands at what we see going on in the world around us and ask, "What are we going to do about . . ."

I believe the answer could be within our very homes. We read about the early church and how they turned their world upside down for Christ. Why can't we do that? What was it about them that made the unbelievers around them marvel? They didn't have mega churches with programs to meet every need. All they had were their homes and they used them. They were known for their hospitality. (Acts 2:42-47) Hospitality was even a requirement to be an elder in the church. The early Christians turned their world upside down with their actions.

I believe that as our culture continues to move more and more in the direction it is heading, very soon we won't be able to ask our acquaintances to merely come to church with us. They will look at us like we've just asked them to go to the moon or to visit some strange cult.

Our culture is crying out for connectedness, and for meaningful, caring relationships; not another meeting. They go to meetings at work and do not want to go to meetings on their time off! Even my adult son once said to me when I was challenging him to go to a Christian conference, "Mom, I don't want to go to a bunch of meetings and have someone lecture me all weekend during my only leisure time."

It is my hope and prayer that this book will motivate you to open your front door, put out the welcome mat, and start inviting your casual acquaintances to your home for some real caring over a cup of coffee or tea. We need to turn our world upside down like the early believers did in the book of Acts:

They broke bread in their homes and ate together with glad and sincere hearts, praising God and enjoying the favor of all the people." Acts 2:46b-47 NIV

> **Our homes and our hospitality are the greatest untapped resource of the church!**

My hope is that this book will help you see entertaining is possible in the midst of your busy schedule.

This book is not meant to be a "Christian" Martha Stewart® book or "How-To" manual. There are plenty of secular books and magazines that can give more ideas than the average woman can possibly do. Those who are more creative and artistic can look to Martha Stewart and others like her for additional help. My prayer is that readers will catch my vision and start to do simple, easy forms of hospitality. I want to free men and women from the compulsion to impress and learn how to use their homes to bring joy and hope to others.

I want to show men and women how they can entertain with ease, forget about the details, and focus on the people God brings across their paths in life. I also want to show them how they can share the love of Jesus Christ and the hope that He gives. A hostess does not have to be a Bible Scholar or a full-time Christian worker to be used by God to bring others to Christ.

Use the tools in this book to open your front door and begin to "give a cup of cold water in Jesus name" to a lonely, harried culture that is in great need of love, genuine friendship and caring. A little "heavenly hospitality" goes a long way. Lives are often changed for all of eternity.

The difference between this book and any other you may pick up on the topic of hospitality is going to be the perspective and underlying reasons for entertaining. The purpose of this book is to show you how easy entertaining can be. You are probably thinking "How can I possibly squeeze entertaining into my busy life!" Maybe you work full time or are single, or you have a house full of children. Maybe your husband works long hours or travels. You may be wondering how you can keep up with your day-to-day responsibilities and still have people into your cluttered home. My hope is that this book will help you see entertaining is possible in the midst of your busy schedule.

Entertaining often says,
"Come on over to my house and let me impress you with what I have and how I do things."

Hospitality says,
"Come on over, just as you are, and be part of our family. There's always room for one more! Kick off your shoes. Make yourself at home."

Your Home

Did you grow up in a home that welcomed people or one in which outsiders were rarely guests? The answer will have affected your desire or willingness to open your own home to others. Ask yourself what is your biggest fear about having guests in your home. Identify the fear and attack it head on. Ask the Lord to show you what you can actively do to overcome any of your fears regarding entertaining and hospitality.

My parents seldom opened our home to guests, but when they did, I was always glad. It added many fond memories to growing up. Hospitality made it to my list of things I wanted to do better, or more often, than my parents. When they entertained, it was always a big deal. Impressing the guests seemed to be a higher value than enjoying them.

However, when I married, I began to observe my gracious mother-in-law, Elisabeth McCullough, who was raised in the South. Her hometown of Charleston, South Carolina has been named the most polite city in America. She came from a large family and was the oldest daughter of a country pastor. Her father often had to serve more than one

congregation. They lived in a tiny manse and were often paid in chickens, pigs and garden produce. Most of her married life was spent as a missionary to the poorest country in South America.

I learned a lot from my mother-in-law. Her home always had an "Open Door" and she graciously served anyone who walked in. She readily made her guests feel at home because she wasn't trying to impress them. She truly cared about them. The moment they walked through her door she made them feel special and they became the center of attention. This genuine compassion flowed from a heart filled with the love of Jesus Christ.

How I got started

As a young woman I struggled with TOTAL commitment to Christ. I wanted to hang on to the "pretty things" of life, afraid that if I gave the Lord EVERYTHING, He would take away all the fun in life. Where that distorted view came from, I don't know, but I will never forget the day I did "battle" over this with the Lord in prayer. It was so hard to surrender the "pretty things" and trust Him to provide for me in my future. Perhaps I had visions of becoming a drab, old-fashioned looking woman who had nothing. I finally decided that God loved me and knew what was best for me in life. In prayer I surrendered and gave him ALL of me and my future and told Him that He came before the "pretty things" of life. When God led my husband and me into full-time Christian work, I told Him I was willing to give up fine china, crystal, nice furniture and a big gorgeous home here on earth for the heavenly mansion he was preparing for me.

When my husband and I were newlyweds, we happily worked for a Christian organization that didn't pay much. The first year on staff we were learning about prerequisites for answered prayer and learned that we have to believe that God will answer our prayer in order to receive the answer to our prayer. (Matthew 21:22)

Driving home to our tiny one-bedroom apartment one day we passed many small ranch-style houses. These were cute, "starter homes" that all looked alike and were placed close together. I sighed and told my husband I didn't want to raise our children in an apartment. I wanted to have a yard for a swing set, and a puppy. I told him that I was going to start praying for a house. Without even turning his head from watching the traffic, he said, "As long as we are in Christian work, we will never own a house."

Determined woman that I am, I refused to believe that. This was to become my first really big challenge to see if God answered "believing prayer." I told him that I was going to ask God to give us a house. I secretly made a "deal" with God and told him that if He gave us a house, I would give it back to him and fill it with His people. I would do anything that would benefit His Kingdom here on earth. For the next three years I quietly prayed that God would provide a house for us before we had children. When I mentioned it to my husband, he would just smile with a look that seemed to say, "Poor girl, this will never happen. I hope it doesn't disappoint her too much."

Finally the time came when "miraculously" the Lord enabled us to buy a house just two blocks from the campus where we worked. As we were walking through the house that was about to become ours, we discovered a workshop in the basement, complete with a workbench for my husband. I turned to him and said, "There dear, look! The Lord has even provided a workshop for you – and you didn't even believe we would own a house."

Our lives and the lives of our family have been greatly enriched by all the wonderful people we have had the privilege of enjoying.

I kept my "deal" with the Lord and immediately began to fill it with the students we worked with, and just about anyone else who came along. As the years have passed, we have lived in five different houses! Each time we moved, I renewed my "deal" with the Lord. The "pretty things" such as fine china and crystal showed up miraculously when they were needed. We have lost track of the number of people who have experienced some sort of hospitality in our homes, having lost our guest book at sometime in our various moves. Our lives and the lives of our family have been greatly enriched by all the wonderful people we have had the privilege of enjoying. I don't know if any of them were literal angels (Hebrews 13:2), but many have come to know the Lord Jesus as their Savior because we opened our home to them.

A perfect example of this is our friend Rich. We had been to a football game with Rich and his sister Linda, a girl in my Bible Study group. She had a burden for her older brother. After the football game, Lynda and I were in my kitchen fixing something to eat. We stood by the sink and prayed quietly together because we overheard my husband, Sam, sharing the Gospel with Rich. We stalled our preparations and were privileged to overhear Rich praying

and asking Christ into his life. We hugged and cried as we stood by the sink that day. Rich went on to become a fully committed follower of Christ. Lynda later went into full-time Christian work and led the rest of her family to the Lord.

A few weeks after we moved into our first house we heard about two students who were brand-new believers. Marta and Toon who were roommates, had been swindled out of their student apartment and were sleeping in various locations – on floors and in broom closets. Being faithful to my "deal" with the Lord, I offered them our guest bedroom even though it was in the midst of having the wallpaper removed, and it only contained a double bed and a desk. They moved in and were a wonderful blessing to us that semester. They later told us that their parents were going to have them leave campus and come home had they not found a place to live. Marta later joined our staff and married a man who was also in full-time Christian work.

You may be thinking, "I'm too private a person. I couldn't do what Nan did." Well, God may not be calling you to take kids in off the street, but He still wants to bless you, using your own talents.

> **Start somewhere, even if it is only inviting someone over for a cup of coffee or tea, and a few words of encouragement.**

Setting the Tone

In setting the tone for your own "heavenly hospitality" it is paramount that you have the right perspective. How you feel about having guests in your home will determine how they feel. Use the tools in this book and open up your home so that you can begin to share the love of Christ with others.

Availability vs. Ability

When you endeavor to be "hospitable" rather than to entertain, you and your guests will be more relaxed. God is not looking for your "ability" but rather your "availability." Jesus himself showed us how to minister in our homes. His first miracle took place at a wedding in Cana. As soon as Matthew came to Christ, he gave a dinner party. Zacchaeus descended the sycamore tree and shared his new-found faith with his guests in his home.

The very fact that you have picked up this book says that you are willing to be available to God and what He may have for you. You are making yourself available to be trained to share your faith. Begin by praying and ask God to show you what He has for you. Our present culture is moving toward more and more isolation. We work at jobs where we sit in cubicles in front of computer screens and talk to unknown faces on telephones. We come home, lock our doors, and sit in front of the television. "Heavenly Hospitality" counteracts this trend because most people are honored when you open your home to them. Titus 1:8 and I Timothy 3:2 say that we must "enjoy" having guests in our home.

I once encouraged a new believer to open her home to her neighbors. Mary had never done anything like this before. I suggested she have a Christmas Coffee, and I would be willing to give a Christmas devotional.

As the neighbors arrived, it was obvious that most of them did not know each other. We asked them to share their own holiday traditions and found that they were eager to share and enjoyed doing so. As the women were leaving the Coffee, they thanked Mary profusely for inviting them into her home and asked her to repeat this event every Christmas! It was clear to see that they were hungry for relationship. From the comments they made we realized that several women had come to a new faith in Jesus after hearing the devotional on the true meaning of Christmas. Mary was on cloud nine. God uses people when they open their homes for "heavenly hospitality."

Fear Phantoms

There are many things that keep people from opening their front doors and taking the risk of extending an invitation. Some of the things people tell themselves are:

"My life is too busy."

"I can't cook well."

"My house is too small or not nice enough."

"I don't have the right dishes or furniture."

"I don't have fancy things."

"It will cost too much."

"No one will want to come."

"I won't know what to say about spiritual things."

"People will think I am a religious 'nut'."

With God's help, you will be able to slay these "dragons" in your life and open your front door to minister in Jesus' name. I have had all those same feelings, especially when we were in our first house. As young newlyweds we did not have the nice china or the crystal. I prayed and the Lord has helped me, He will help you, too. This book is designed to give you the tools you need to get started. You will be able to see how easy it can be.

The next time you doubt your ability to use your home as a ministry, turn to the Word of God in your "Quiet Time" with the Lord. Here are some verses to use as you prayerfully prepare for your part in "heavenly hospitality."

Feeling inadequate?

Philippians 4:13
Jeremiah 33:3
Matthew 7:7
I Thessalonians 5:24
Philippians 4:19
II Corinthians 12:9

Feeling scared?

Psalm 34:4
I Peter 5:7
Proverbs 3:5, 6
Ephesians 6:10, 11
Deuteronomy 20:3, 4
Isaiah 26:3

Additional verses are listed in the final chapter of this book.

You may not have the spiritual gift of hospitality but all of us are commanded in scriptures to practice it. Even the great apostle Paul often asked for prayer so that he would be bold and would be used by the Lord. He said that he came in fear and trembling, not using lofty words. Remember, God is not asking you to be Emily Post or Martha Stewart. He merely asks us to open the door to our homes, commit it to Him and He will do the rest. He is not asking for ability but availability. As I have had the privilege of seeing lives changed because I was available, I have been amazed that God can use me. Acts 20:24 LB has become my life's verse: "My life is worth NOTHING unless I use it for the work assigned me by the Lord Jesus Christ; the work of telling others the Good News about God's mighty kindness and love."

Attitude Check
What is the greatest thing that has ever happened to you? What is the greatest thing that you could do for another person? The answer to both of these questions should be a personal encounter with Christ. Focus on simply sharing the love of Christ with your guests rather than trying to impress them with your domestic skills.

Being both Mary and Martha

Most of us are familiar with the Biblical story of Mary and Martha from Luke 10:38-42. While each of us tends to be like one or the other of these women, our attitude should be a combination of both Mary and Martha. I am like Martha, and my sister-in-law, Ann Schwab, is like Mary. Martha-types can beat themselves up because it appears that Jesus favored Mary, but remember the whole picture! As we read through the Gospels we will notice whose house Jesus chose as the home base for his ministry. It must have been a home of order and organization. I happen to think that it was because Martha applied her practical skills and wisdom, along with Mary's warm touch with people. Martha made it easy for Jesus and his disciples to minister. She had her house in order and they could count on her.

Martha and I are kindred spirits. We tend to get the job done and done well. We fuss over the details of "things" rather than people. Mary, on the other hand focused on people. She may have been disorganized at times, but people who entered her door absolutely loved her and knew that they were loved.

Whether you are a Mary or a Martha, single or married, apartment dweller or homeowner, in a big city or a small town, you can use whatever the Lord has blessed you with in showing "heavenly hospitality." If the Lord Jesus is invited and the Holy Spirit is moving, it will be a success.

What kind of home is needed?

Remember that your home is a gift from God and belongs to Him. Use what He has blessed you with for His glory. Never apologize for God's gift to you. If you are a good steward of what He has blessed you with, He will multiply it.

I've watched my missionary sister-in-law turn "shabby chic" into a style. Even in a humble missionary apartment with patches sewn on her sofa, she used someone's leftover unmatched dishes and set her table with cute homemade decorations. Do not fall into the comparison trap! The apostle Paul said he learned to be content whether he had a lot or a little. (Philippians 4:12) Ask God to give you this attitude and let go of comparisons. Have the same attitude of Christ who gave up all the riches of glory to minister to us with the attitude of a servant. (Philippians 2:5-11)

Arrange the rooms in your house in a comfortable manner so that you can concentrate on your guests and their needs. Focus on your guests by practicing the Golden Rule: "Do unto others as you would have them do unto you." Remember, it is not about you!

Your home does not have to be the kind that is featured in an article in "House Beautiful" magazine in order for you to offer "heavenly hospitality." You also do not want to send your family into a "tail spin" just because you are having guests. Get everyone on board by giving them responsible ownership in the event. In this way, they won't resent the fact that outsiders are coming over. Begin with prayer for the people you have invited, and then ask each family member to help get the house ready.

Start by living an orderly lifestyle. Get in the habit of picking up around the house as you go. Try your hand at multi-tasking. When you find yourself on the telephone for longer than a quick call, do some picking up. If you have little children, you may feel that this is an impossible task, but by making picking up a part of your daily routine, you will not be too far behind when someone knocks at your door.

When my children were little, I read Karen Main's book, Open Home, Open Heart. It released me from trying to impress others. Karen told a story of a woman who came to her door with a need for counsel. Karen's little boy's Matchbox cars were strewn all over the house. The visiting woman never noticed or

cared! After reading that book, I changed my perspective. Whenever I would look around at the chaos and toys, I would ask myself, "Are you getting ready for Better Homes and Gardens to come for pictures, or are you raising three kids?" That was always a good reality check to get me back to the real world.

My children also helped me with my perspective. One evening on the way home from visiting another family's home, our children were happily discussing how much fun they had. I asked them what they thought of the family's "messy" house, even listing several rooms that were out of order. My children were much more impressed with how much fun they had in those messy rooms and what a great family they were. That settled it for me. They showed me what was really important and what is noticed by most people. The better question to ask is, "Were personal needs met there and were people ministered to?

Included in the reference section are several web sites that will help you with home organization like www.flylady.com

Welcoming Details

Consider the entrance to your home. Is it welcoming? You want your guests to feel welcome from the moment they arrive. Sweep off the front stoop and put a pot of flowers or ivy on the porch. Dust off the cobwebs around the door. Buy a seasonal decoration or a wreath at the local craft store and hang it on the front door. This seems to say "We are expecting you and are excited that you are here!"

Make sure your front light is on and the house numbers are easily seen at any time of day. Consider putting your outdoor lights on a timer (available at home improvement stores) so that they are always on from dusk until 10 or 11 o'clock at night.

For large gatherings, you might lead the way to your home with balloons or signs. When your guests approach your mailbox or lantern and notice the balloons tied on, not only will they know that they are at the right house, but they will also anticipate the fun they are about to have. Your sign could say "The Party's Here!" If you have a screen or storm door, leave your front door ajar which seems to say "You are at the right place and we are expecting you!"

WELCOME!
Come on in.

You might also put a 4 x 6" card on the front door that reads "Welcome. Come on in!" This is especially helpful for late-arriving guests when you are busy with others and cannot be at the door any longer.

A Welcoming Host

Be at the door, not in the kitchen, when guests arrive. From the moment they arrive, your purpose should be to make them feel special and comfortable.

Aim: *Make your guests feel comfortable and very special*

- Help guests with their coats. Clear out the hall closet and have plenty of hangers available or purchase an inexpensive coat rack and put it in a nearby bedroom.
- Introduce your guests to each other. Consider using name tags for a large crowd of people.
- Make sure the guests know ahead of time what the attire will be so they will feel appropriately dressed.
- Offer your guests something to drink, even if it is just a glass of water.
- Try to be at the door as guests leave so you can thank them for coming.

"Unexpected Guest" tips

It is important that they too feel cared for and that they matter. Welcome them warmly. Offer them something to drink. Never apologize for the condition of your home.

Preparing Heavenly Rooms that affect Eternity

The Home

Keep things simple. Remember that you are not trying to impress but rather to help your guests have a memorable experience. Use what you already have as much as possible. I still marvel when people remark, "Your home is so warm and cozy" even when I have done nothing fancy. My home is decorated with things that mean something to our family. Your home should be a reflection of you. If our homes belong to the Lord Jesus Christ, they should also be a reflection of a gracious, generous, loving God who blesses. Our homes should woo people to the Savior.

We want them to go home thinking, "There was something special there and I want to know more about it."

Billy Graham's wife, Ruth, said, "No matter what the size of one's home, it can and should be a welcoming place. Whether a cottage or a mansion, if loving hearts live there, it will show in the family pictures, the old loved books, and the bits and pieces of treasures accumulated through the years."

Architect Georg Andersen's book, <u>Silent Witness, the Language of Your Home</u> examines what a home reveals about our priorities, faith, and purpose in life. He says, "We can minister without words to everyone who graces our doorstep. Let the spirit of your home speak to all who enter."

Room Prep Tips

Use what the Lord has given you. You do not need money or fancy things. Give your home to Him and watch Him bless you for it. No home is too small. For a small group, confine the gathering to one or two rooms by arranging the furniture and food there. Close the doors of the rooms where you do not want your guests to go. For large events, open up as much as you can and move or remove furniture. In warm weather or climates, open up to the out-of-doors. Use your lawn, patio or deck. Anticipate the flow of traffic. Adjust your thermostat for guests. Rooms heat up when crowded.

Living Rooms and Family Rooms

Most houses have family rooms and living rooms. I have always chuckled at the name "living room". It seems like a misnomer. No one lives in that room. It is more like the old fashioned parlor so I use it that way. I keep it picked up and ready at a moment's notice for drop-in guests. The kids have to relegate their toys, sporting gear and school papers to other rooms; preferably their bedrooms. The operative words for the living room are "use it!" I use it for a quick "tea for two", a spur-of-the-moment prayer meeting with someone who drops in with a need, or for Bible study groups and times when I want privacy from the rest of the family. They can go on with their lives in the family room.

Some homes only have one room for gathering. Whichever you have, make the most of the room and make it homey with pictures and knick-knacks that mean something to you and your family. Make sure you hang your pictures close to the furniture so they look connected. Arrange the furniture in a manner that allows good conversation. Bring extra chairs in for larger crowds. If you own your home and can paint, make sure the colors you choose make the room inviting. Paint cool colors on the sunny side of the house and warm colors on the dark side of the house. Warm colors create a festive mood and cool colors are soothing and relaxing.

Light a few scented candles or votives. Turn soft music on. Background piano or flute has a calming effect. If you have a fireplace, use it. Light a fire in the fireplace on chilly days, not just in the evenings.

One time my guests came in and happily announced that they could smell the fire in my fireplace when they got out of their car. They said it welcomed them and made them excited about coming in.

Keep your coat closet tidy, leaving space for guests to hang their coats. For large events, clear out the coat closet or set up an inexpensive coat rack in a nearby room. Keep your "Welcome, Come on In" sign taped to the inside of your closet door. That way you will always have it and know where it is.

Tip

Use commercial "3 hour logs" and pile a few pieces of wood on top; that way the fire crackles and looks warm and inviting. You will not have to tend to it after your guests arrive.

The Bathroom or Powder Room

Make sure someone wipes the bathroom up the day of the event. Keep boxes of pop-up sanitizing wipes under the vanity for this sort of thing. Remember to touch up the mirror. Keep basic cleaning supplies in each bathroom under the sink for quick touch ups. Check the toilet paper and have extra rolls in sight especially if a group of women are coming. You can put them in a decorative basket on the floor near the toilet. You might even want to put a few feminine sanitary products discreetly in the same basket for a guest's emergency.

Hand towels are another issue. For most small events make sure there are a couple of clean hand towels hanging on the towel bar. Keep these separate from the "family towel". Some people prefer the pricier paper type but children can make a mess of them. A cheaper alternative is to put a supply of finger tip towels in a neat pile on the vanity or roll up several wash cloths in a basket with another basket on the floor for the used ones to be tossed. Put away personal items and light a scented candle. Put out a fresh bar of soap or use liquid soap in a pump. If your house has a lot of doors, consider putting a sign which says "Restroom" on the bathroom door.

Keep this taped to the inside door of the vanity and put it out on the door on the day of the event.

Bathroom Basket

- Extra toilet paper
- Extra finger tip towels
- Feminine sanitary supplies
- Christian devotional, poem booklet or Christian magazine

- Secure your hair so as not to find any in the food later
- Wash hands thoroughly
- Do as much as you can ahead of time. Use make-ahead recipes.
- Before cookouts, be sure you have gas for the grill
- Recheck your ingredients ahead of time to be sure you have everything the recipes call for.
- Check your ice supply

Tip

Only keep things on your counter that you use every day. That way it will not look cluttered and you will have room for serving.

Kitchen

The next room to consider is the "nerve center" of the home, the kitchen. People naturally gravitate there. Unless you have someone to welcome them, and to keep your guests busy in the living room, count on them migrating into your kitchen. Often I serve appetizers at the kitchen bar and then we move into the dining room for the meal. This is a good reason to try to keep counters cleaned up.

If you have done all your prep work, welcoming your guests is easier. If possible, wash up mixing bowls, pots & pans before guests arrive so that after dinner, all you have to do is load the dishwasher. This "clean as you go" style will also enable you to go to bed earlier.

An organized kitchen keeps you from being frazzled. It also makes it easy for friends to help you with your events. Set up your cabinets and drawers so that they make sense and have "centers" for various activities. For example, keep all your supplies for putting leftovers away in one "center" so that a helper can easily put food away while you scrape dishes and load the dishwasher.

Set up a station for coffee and beverages so that guests can help themselves. Keep mugs and coffee supplies in the cabinet nearest the coffee maker. The cold beverage station should be near the refrigerator or you can set out an ice bucket and glasses on the counter with drinks in cans or bottles and a pitcher of water so guests can help themselves. Remember to put some cocktail napkins on your counter. You might wish to have your husband or a friend act as "bartender," offering drinks and setting out the appetizers while you put the finishing touches on the meal. This is especially helpful when having a potluck and you need to be free to accept food as it arrives.

Clean as you go tips to remember

- Buy a brush on a stick that dispenses dish detergent. Great for quick wash ups of your prep items.

- Have a pan or bowl of soapy water in your sink and use that as you work in the kitchen. Place items on a drainer or towel and put them away before your guests arrive.

Work Smart!

Never work over an open drawer. There is nothing worse than spilling something in your silverware drawer just before you need to set your table!

Top Tips

- PREPARE as much as you can as far ahead as you can.
- STICKY NOTE PADS: Write things down as you think of them and put notes where it will help you remember details.
- CLEAN AS YOU GO whether pots and pans or powder rooms so you are always ready.
- COOK & SERVE in the same container.
- MULTI-TASK as much as you can but never at the expense of "people".
- STOCK PANTRY OR FREEZER with last minute items for unexpected guests: cookies, canned fruit for salad, a main dish casserole, and frozen lasagna

Well Stocked Pantry and Freezer

I will always remember the evening I had forgotten that our campus Villanova University staff team was coming for dinner. I was a busy mom with a baby and a toddler. I was standing in the kitchen when I heard a knock at the door. Glancing out the window I saw the whole team standing on the front steps. Panicking, I called Sam to quickly answer the door while I flew into high gear preparing a spaghetti dinner. I explained that I was running behind and Sam served them beverages, cheese, and crackers while I opened cans of tomatoes and boiled water. Everyone cheerfully pitched in setting the table and a wonderful evening followed with lots of laughter and rich conversation.

Another time a wedding party arrived straight from the airport to meet for the rehearsal with my husband. I realized that they needed some refreshments first. So for a quick punch, I grabbed my "ever-ready" frozen ice ring and literally threw it into the punch bowl along with a can of undiluted frozen lemonade and equal parts of cranberry juice and ginger ale from the pantry. I popped a frozen pizza into the oven and cut it into appetizer-size pieces for them. I laid all this out on my kitchen island along with cocktail napkins and soon stomachs were no longer growling and the rehearsal plans could go on.

Self-Locking Plastic Storage Bags

These are fabulous for helping you keep organized probably second only to sticky note pads. They come in almost any size. Use them for:

- Sorting seasonal table decorations like napkin rings and centerpiece items
- Storing place cards
- Keeping table linens clean and ready
- Saving food prep time by storing diced or pre-sliced recipe items
- Marinating meats
- Piping icing or sauces (cut off the corner of bag and squeeze)
- Storing leftovers or sending leftovers home with guests
- Holding ice cubes in freezer in order to have extras on hand
- Having ice in baggies for easy removal of wax or gum
- Crushing crackers or cookies for recipes (smash with mallet or rolling pin)

A well stocked pantry will set you free to be ready for drop-in guests at anytime. There are a few basic items that you can keep on hand. You should have some beverages, special cookies, a quick dessert and ingredients to prepare an emergency dinner.

My children used to refer to my fancy Pepperidge Farm's cookies as "grown up cookies" that they knew not to touch. I always had a package of something like this on hand so I was always ready to offer a surprise guest a cup of coffee or tea with a special treat.

You might want to keep a reserve stock of "company drinks" that are off limits to any family member who may go foraging through your pantry. These might be something like Coke®, Diet Coke®, and Sprite®. In the summer keep instant ice tea and instant lemonade on hand for unexpected guests.

I always have a box of chocolate cake mix, instant chocolate pudding and chocolate chips for my "Fast Fixin' Chocolate Cake" recipe, which can be made in the cake pan and does not need frosting. It goes together in a flash.

For an emergency dinner, I keep a large-sized frozen lasagna in my freezer as well as the ingredients to make spaghetti in my pantry. Sometimes I freeze some browned ground beef, ground turkey or onions in a self-locking freezer bag in my freezer. This can be used for the spaghetti or a lot of other quick dishes. Frozen meatballs can be bought commercially and kept on hand for emergencies.

See the recipes section, pg 225 to learn how to make Nan's "Fast Fixin' Chocolate Cake"

The following list will help you be prepared for drop-in guests. Have a list of things that you enjoy making and always keep the necessary ingredients on hand.

Cranberry juice
Frozen ice ring for punch bowl
Frozen lemonade, ginger ale and colas
Crackers
Jar of soft spread cheese
Mixed Nuts
Salsa & Chips
Soups: mushroom, tomato, cream of chicken,
        2 cans of a gourmet soup
Instant rice
Instant potatoes
Seasoning mixes for chili and for tacos
Gourmet spaghetti sauce
Spaghetti noodles
Frozen lasagna
Frozen ground beef or chicken already
        cooked & microwave ready
Frozen meat balls
Frozen grated cheddar cheese
Quick mixes for muffins, corn bread, banana
        bread and biscuits
Some sort of easy box mix dessert like
        brownies, bars or cookies
Cans of fruit like mandarin oranges, pineapple
        chunks, maraschino cherries and
        coconut for a quick salad
Paper products: plates, cups, and napkins

Tip:

Use a bundt® pan or tupperware to freeze an ice ring the right size for your punch bowl. This will melt slower than ice cubes and will not water down your punch.

DINING ROOM

Like your living room, try to keep your dining room picked up and ready. The table can easily become a dumping ground for papers, mail, etc. If you make the effort to keep it picked up, having people over for a meal does not require so much preparation. Use your good china, too. What are you saving it for?

I have lived in all styles of houses and the separate dining room or separate living room may look elegant but is really impractical. The optimum room arrangement in a house is to have the dining room open into the living room. Now you can expand a large meeting into the dining room or expand a large dinner into the living room. For showers, "heavenly hospitality events," or even a neighborhood meeting, try taking all the leaves out of the dining table and push it against a wall.

If you do that, you can seat large groups of people and still serve food buffet style from the table. Sometimes for very large groups, I will put some of the living room furniture in a bedroom or the garage and put up a second dining room table in the living room. This has enabled me to have a sit down dinner for as many as 28. Lap trays are nice for crowds but can sometimes be awkward and difficult to handle.

You may not be handy or you may live in a rented home. Make the most of what the Lord has given you. Your dining room does not have to be fancy. Even a plain tablecloth and simple centerpiece can be sufficient when the chatter and laughter around the table are rich and joyous. For the first years of marriage we only had an old drop-leaf table and three chairs that matched. My college bookcase served as my "side board" displaying my wedding gifts.

You may be wondering how I can seat 28 people at tables! Most of the time my dining room table is topped with a 4' x 8' piece of 3/4" plywood. My husband rounded off the corners with a small saw and I covered the bare wood with contact paper to make it smooth. A long piece of fabric from the fabric store or a "banquet" size tablecloth covers this large table. Now I can easily seat 12 - 14 people. This has worked so well that we use a second 4' x 8' plywood board on an old table or my picnic table. I put this second 4' x 8' table in my living room. When not in use, we keep these table tops against the wall in our garage or basement.

Tip:

If you move your dining room table, don't forget to shorten the chain of the chandelier so guests won't hit their heads! Use a large paper clip bent in a "S" shape to shorten the chain.

Tabletop Tip:

Take a 4' x 8' Sheet of ¾" plywood and round the corners and put on top of your dining room table.

Chapter 2

Enjoy Entertaining for Eternity with Easy Planning

When you entertain for Eternity with heavenly hospitality, you will want to spend <u>less</u> time working at entertaining and <u>more</u> time enjoying your guests. If you are at ease, then the Lord can easily shine through you and your event.

Like any successful event, a good gathering - especially an easy one - takes planning. But that's where the fun starts. The Lord can use just about anything if it is committed to him. Think about a time you enjoyed a gathering in your past as you try some of the ideas in this book. Combine the best of both worlds.

Your event should be as formal or informal as are the people you are inviting. What will make them comfortable? There's a difference between having your softball team over and having a group of CEOs. The goal is to allow your guests to feel at home and be free to encounter the Lord at your event. Remember that you can use your home, an apartment community room, a club or maybe even your office for larger events.

Consider which venue will be the best situation for what you want to accomplish or for the particular group of people you are entertaining. Use the KISS principle: "**K**eep **I**t **S**imple **S**weetie". If it becomes too complicated, you won't feel like doing the event or will be so frazzled that you won't be able to minister to your guests.

For some occasions, fine china may be nice but you do not need it. Your everyday dishes will do just fine. For other occasions colorful paper products will be perfect. Use what the Lord has blessed you with. Look around at what you have and be creative. There's a big difference between a formal tea and a picnic and there are a lot of variations in between.

Go to the book's web site www.EntertainingForEternity.com and in the community blog section tell others what worked for you and learn what worked for others.

The KISS principle:

Keep
It
Simple
Sweetie

Decide The Details
· What · When · Where · How ·

Ask the Lord to show you where to begin and to give you His perspective. Ask Him to set you free from yourself and to help you relax and enjoy using your home for Him. Ask the Holy Spirit to empower you and your event. Let the love of Christ shine through. Decide up front that this is going to be fun and not frantic. When you are excited about what you're doing or love the reason you're doing it, you will exude confidence and enthusiasm, and people will notice. "Enthusiasm" comes from two Greek words that mean "God within". Consequently, the only truly enthusiastic people are those who have Christ living within them! Your events will have a totally different "feel" from other events that people attend because of your enthusiasm.

I'll never forget the comment made by a congressman after coming to his first Christian Embassy event. We had invited a Christian psychologist to speak on the topic of balancing family life and work. At the end of the evening the congressman shook our hands and said, "Thank you so much for inviting me tonight! It was a truly stimulating evening! How refreshing it was to be at an event where someone doesn't want something from me but rather offers something of substance to me!"

With some careful planning and thinking, you, too, can have events that will not only be memorable but meaningful. Your events will leave people thinking about eternal and important life issues and wanting to come back again.

A few details to consider:

- · Purpose
- · Theme
- · Guests
- · Name tags
- · Invitations
- · Decorations
- · Serving style
- · Room arrangement
- · Menu

Pick a Purpose and Theme

Parties with a purpose

Perhaps there have been times when you have gone to a function out of social obligation. Sometimes you come home thinking: "Why did we go to that?" or "I wish we had stayed home." Then there have been times when you have attended something and it has been a pleasant surprise and you were so very glad you made the effort to go. The scriptures teach us that whatever we do we should "do to the glory God" and that things should be done with excellence. You want your guests to feel glad they came as they drive home. You want them thinking, "I want to go to their house again sometime."

Decide whether your gathering is going to be a <u>Fellowship</u>, <u>Relational</u> or <u>Invitational</u> Event.

> ## <u>Fellowship</u>
> means that your guests are believers and your purpose will be to build up or encourage them.

> ## <u>Relational</u>
> events are to build positive relationships with those who do not know the Lord and maybe have never experienced his love.

> ## <u>Invitational</u>
> events are meant to present the Gospel in a clear and relevant manner. Do not let this style scare you. The latter half of this book will give you specific ideas and themes for your events and show you how to do this successfully.

Let the occasion dictate the format of your event. Even showers, engagement parties, graduations, anniversaries, special birthdays and other celebrations can take on one or more of these styles.

Several years ago I was asked to give a little devotional at a shower for a friend's future daughter-in-law. I had pictured this event as being "fellowship" but as my friend met me at the door she was all excited and concerned. She had learned that some of the bridesmaids did not know the Lord.

Right on the spot my friend asked me if I could make my devotional more relevant to the group. My talk was going to be about finding fulfillment in life by looking to the Lord rather than to your husband to be your Prince Charming. I changed a few sentences and included an opportunity to ask Jesus to be your Prince Charming and Lord of your life. Instantly the event went from fellowship to invitational. The bridesmaids were so curious about the new perspective on marriage that they asked the bride more about me. As a result, after the honeymoon we began a Bible study and several of the bridesmaids came to know Christ personally.

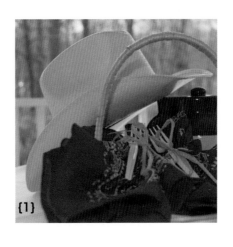

{1}

{2}

{6}

{9}

{10}

{11}

Themes

Themes can be a lot of fun no matter what the occasion! Be creative and let yourself try some new things. This book offers several ideas to try but don't just be limited to these. Our web site will have new ideas that will be constantly added and updated. Use the community blog section and report back about things you've tried that were a success. Theme events don't have to be elaborate, expensive or time consuming. These types of events can set your event apart from the "usual" occasions people attend and will send your guest home with fond memories and a desire to come again.

Here are some examples of themes:

{1} Texas or Western Barbeque: When you invite your guests, suggest that they wear western-style clothing. Use bandanas as decorations, and play country music in the background.

{2} Hawaiian Luau: Provide plastic or silk floral leis and have guests wear Island print shirts and muumuus. Play Hawaiian music in the background

{3} Princess Party: See the Children's chapter for ideas

{4} 50's, 60's or 70's Party: Encourage your guests to go to thrift shops to find 50's, 60's or 70's era clothing. Wear hair styles of the era and play music from the era.

{5} Ethnic or International: Include Italian, German, Spanish, etc.

{6} Chinese New Year: Celebrate the Chinese New Year in late January with Chinese food and Asian decorations.

{7} TV driven event: Super Bowl Party (or other big games), Academy Awards, Miss America Pageant or Election Night. Use the "hot" show to gather friends together. Rent a projection device to show the event on a wall if you do not have a large screen TV.

{8} Wedding Movies Night: Have guests bring their wedding albums or video. Serve a mock wedding cake to enjoy as you laugh together and share how you met.

{9} Ice Cream Social: Provide the beverage and ice cream and have guests bring toppings.

{10} Salad Bar Luncheon: Provide the lettuce, dressing and bread. Guests bring a random addition like cherry tomatoes, diced veggies, grated cheese, etc.

{11} Impromptu Bad Weather Party: Have neighbors over for potluck when you are snowbound.

Organizing and How-to Tips

Throughout this book you will find lots of very practical tips and charts that will make Entertaining for Eternity EASY! Watch for the text tips and check out the charts and resources in the back of the book and on the web site. Be as organized as you can. It will set self-styled Marthas free to be more like Mary. It will help you better meet the physical needs of your guests. The most important thing is to get started as early as you can with your planning. Enlist help from others.

Don't try to do everything yourself or at the last minute.

One morning a friend arrived early at my house for Bible Study. As she watched me put the finishing touches on the refreshments, she asked, "Is having us here every week causing you too much work?" I knew she had asked this because she has a difficult time keeping her household organized.

I assured her with a ready answer of, "No, not at all. In fact it's not a problem. I rather enjoy having the women in my home." The reason I can say that is because I have learned over the years to live in a relatively organized manner so that I can put something together without much effort. My number one principle is always to be picking up things as I walk through my house and to do two things at once whenever I can. Then I do as much as I can as far ahead as possible.

The key to planning is "write it down, write it down, write it down!" I live by sticky note pads. I do not know what I would do without them. I keep them in the kitchen, by the phone, on my desk and beside my bed. Whenever I think of something that needs to be done, I write it down. If the idea is for the menu, I take the note to the kitchen and post it on the refrigerator. If it's someone I need to call, I put the note by the phone. If it's something to buy, I put the note on my wallet in my purse. To remind myself to clean the powder room mirror, I put a sticky note right on that mirror saying: "Clean for neighborhood coffee". Sometimes I even get lucky and my husband sees it and does it!

Write it down, write it down, write it down!

Instructions for Helpers

Make it easy for people to help you by using the sticky note pads. Write down tasks or indicate where you want them to set out items. If you keep a 3 x 5" card in your silverware drawer showing a simple drawing of how to set the table, your children (no matter what age) can help you set the table. Older children can fill the water glasses or make the place cards. I still have some of the place cards my daughter made. They are a special treasure and fond remembrance. Put sticky notes on serving plates so others will know where you want the food put and so you will remember to put out all of the food.

Write down your menu and post it on the refrigerator door so others can help you. That will also be a good reminder to you so you won't forget anything. Keep a record of who came for dinner along with the date and put the old cards together somewhere to check the next time you have them over. That way you won't end up serving them the same thing. It will also become an idea file of sorts.

Event Check List

Set a definite date and place for your event.

Secure your speaker (if appropriate).

Print your invitations.

Deliver or mail your invitations at least 7-10 days prior to the event

Arrange for childcare if necessary, and put away pets.

Prepare food ahead of time.

Decorate your home appropriate to the time of year.

Make reminder phone calls to guests.

Make name tags.

If you have a speaker, call them to go over details.

Decide what you are going to do for follow up of your event (informal personal appointments or a simple group Bible Study).

Make sure the room is set up properly and all phones are turned off.

Ask one or two people to pray during your event (if appropriate).

Prepare Comment Cards, pencils, and a basket to collect them (see pg 192 for an explanation of Comment Cards).

Select appropriate background music.

Get everything done ahead of time and take a deep breath. Pray with your speaker so you are ready to greet your guests and give them your full attention.

Preparing Your Family for Special Dinners or Parties

- Plan what you each will wear the day before
- Launder and lay out family clothes ahead of time
- Have everyone dressed befotre the last minute
- Pray together for the event
- Pass out "Help Assignment Lists"

Learn from Others

Ask an older or more experienced woman to mentor you. Most of my hospitality skills were learned by observing older, wiser women like my mother, my mother-in-law, or various women from the many churches we've attended. My Irish Aunt Betty and my Southern Aunt Marion have also been good role models. Pastors' wives have often been a great resource and they have great recipes, too.

My mother taught me refined social skills and class. My mother-in-law taught me godly, southern charm. Women in older generations can teach us much. These are women who practiced what is fast becoming a lost art.

While my mom "entertained," my husband's mom practiced "hospitality". Going to an all-girls finishing school taught my mother how to be proper when entertaining. My mother-in-law practiced hospitality even living in a mud hut among the Quechua Indians. After all those early years in Bolivia, Mom McCullough came home and became a pastor's wife and later my father-in-law was the Director of the Mission. Sunday dinner was never "just family" at their house.

I still remember the first time I went home with Sam to meet his parents. I thought, "Wow! Real live, mud-hut missionaries!" I was intimidated and a little unsure of myself. As we came in the door, she dropped everything that she was doing and came up to me and gave me a warm, welcoming hug saying in her heavy southern drawl, "I declare! We are so glad to meet you and have you in our home!

Sam has talked about you so much. We could hardly wait to meet you."

Simple but tasty food, rich conversations and lots of laughter is what I remember of her home. Often we sat around a table that would never have made the cover of a magazine. Her hand-me-down dishes were barely noticed because the love flowed and laugher filled the air.

After Sam and I were married, we began to speak in churches and at missions conferences. We always seemed to meet people who knew Sam's parents. NEVER was there anything but gushing praise said about them. So as I began to quietly watch and observe, I thought, "Why is it that everyone just loves them so much? What can I learn from them?" They were far from wealthy. She had none of the fancy things that my mom had, yet people would tell me that they would never forget being in her home. I observed her and asked many questions as I helped her in the kitchen.

Find an older, more experienced woman to observe. Do not be too shy to ask someone to mentor you. Offer to help when they have guests and learn all you can. The Bible admonishes older women to train the younger women in their home skills. Titus 2:5 says to be "...self-controlled...pure... busy at home [and] kind...". Not only will you be blessed by spending time with an older woman, but her life will be enriched by spending time with you!

Let Others Help

Do not be afraid to enlist the help of other friends in hosting an event. Get your guests involved in some of the fun and anticipation by assigning tasks. The mood catches on and others start adding their ideas to yours. Consequently, you are not left with all the work.

One new guest who had never been to my home arrived early to observe two of my girlfriends helping me set up and work in the kitchen. We were having such fun together getting ready that my new guest remarked, "Wow! I never thought of getting friends to help me entertain! You are having so much fun! I thought I always had to do everything myself."

Family Helpers

You cannot do everything by yourself. Sometimes friends remark that they cannot believe how much I get done but I have to give my husband a lot of credit. We work as a team and celebrate each other's gifts. I could not do half of what I do if it was not for him. He can't and won't cook but he makes great invitations, name tags or place cards on a computer and is very personable with our guests. He's very supportive of women's events, too. When the children were at home they each had a little job to contribute to all our meals and helped at our events. Write jobs down on cards and pass them out to your "helpers". Develop specific jobs that a family member can individually own and be responsible for. Keep your standard job cards in a kitchen drawer so they are handy when someone asks, "Can I help you?"

Husband List

- Come home from work early to help
- Prepare beverages: prepare to serve drinks when they first arrive, put water & ice in glasses, make coffee
- Select background music and light candles. Consider other lighting needs
- Help wash dishes
- Help greet at the door

Children's List

- Set the table
- Make the place cards
- Place the water pitcher on the table
- Pour the water into the glasses before guests arrive
- Clear the table

Guests

Choose
The first person to invite to your event is Jesus! Think and pray about who you should invite to your event. Be open to the Holy Spirit's prompting. Generally, it's nice that the guests have something in common but sometimes a mixed group makes interesting conversation. Start with a group such as neighbors, co-workers, club members, classmates or teammates. As you pray, keep a list and write down names as they come to you. The key to an event's success is the prayer behind it rather than great planning or fabulous food.

Schedule
Next, think about a day of the week and time of the day that would be conducive to the maximum number of people on your list. Take into consideration holidays and school vacations.

Details
Decide if it will be for women only or couples or families. A Mother-Daughter Tea can be an enjoyable event and can be excellent way to teach your daughter how to share her faith. If it's for couples, make sure that your husband is available to participate.

Children
If your guests have children, you will have to consider childcare, especially if you are having a direct presentation of the Gospel. For a daytime Coffee, you may want to secure a neighbor's home for childcare and arrange for a babysitter. Children can be a welcome addition to some events, but they can be a distraction at others. On the other hand, at some family or holiday events, children can be more easily tuned in to spiritual aspect than their parents may be. On several occasions, children have asked some very good questions during an event. Often children can be the gateway to opening up a whole family to Christ and the Gospel.

Before the collapse of Communism, there was a diplomatic family that had defected from their communist country. They came to our home frequently during their transition time in the "safe house". Often, we served a simple meal like pizza. We had no idea what they were thinking regarding spiritual things. We shared our lives and the Gospel with them as best we could. Finally, they moved into their own home and invited us over for dinner. After we all were seated, the wife turned to my husband, Sam, and said, "Will you do it?" Puzzled, Sam asked her what she meant. She said that since coming to our house and observing our mealtime blessing, their youngest child had asked them to do the same. You never know what children will pick up or how it will affect the whole family for eternity.

Guest Lists

Who you will include will be determined by the purpose of your event. The important operative here is to cover each invitee with prayer. Consider your guest list a prayer list also. Make two copies of your guest list. Keep one where it will remind you to pray for them, perhaps in your Bible. Keep another list by your telephone and record the R.S.V.P.s. Be sure your husband and children mark down responses if they answer the phone. Get the family involved in praying for them, too. It will add an air of expectation and get them more excited to see what the Lord is going to do.

Enjoy making your guest list. This is your opportunity to invite your favorite people or those you've always wanted to get to know better. Think through the various groups of people you and your family bump into regularly: teams, clubs, scouts, work.

Create Interesting Mixes of Guests

Be sensitive to how various personality types will interact, but don't be afraid to let the Holy Spirit work his wonders. In our frantic world, many people seldom get invited to events with heavenly hospitality. Often, social occasions are business related or social obligations. For many believers and unbelievers alike, your event may provide one of the few times they get out and meet new people. Take a chance and mix it up, inviting believers and non-believers. After you commit your event to the Lord, stand back and marvel at how the Lord leads and moves among your guests. What fun!

When you are planning your seating arrangement, consider a balance among your guests. At a sit-down table event, seat the extroverts next to the shy people. Mix the men and women up so the men don't end up at one end of the table talking only football. Remember, too, that in most couples it is the woman who is the more social and talkative. Mixing it up will help keep the conversations lively and moving. Mix up different age groups, too. The young and the old can learn a lot from each other.

Match your number of guests to your occasion, your budget, and the capacity of your home.

Remember
rule of thumb:

Invite 3 times the number of people that you expect to come to your event.

Name Tags

Use your R.S.V.P. list as you make name tags and place cards. Some people feel name tags are not necessary but they do help put the guests at ease. They are for <u>their</u> benefit -- not yours. They also help your speaker and the group to interact. Most people are not particularly good at remembering names. Write large and legibly. This will also help you know who has not arrived yet. Name tags can be colorful and fun. Try putting stickers on them if you like instead of computer art.

Remembering names shows you care about people

Remembering Names

Ask for the name

> Most people probably do not hear the name in the first place. Be sure to listen intently while being introduced. Think of someone else you know with the same name and that association will help you remember the new friend.

Repeat the name

> By repeating the name, you impress it on your memory. You may even ask how it is spelled. Use it often in the ensuing conversation.

Look intently at their name tag.

> This will help you make a mental image.

Write down the name

> As soon as you can, write down the name, perhaps on a scrap of paper in your purse or pocket. Business cards are a great help. Offer yours and maybe they will have one also.

Being a Good Guest

Perhaps <u>you</u> are unaccustomed to being a guest in someone's home. Here are a few suggestions you might use when you are invited to a social event. First of all, remember the Golden Rule:

"Do unto others as you would have them do unto you!"

- Be prompt in responding to R.S.V.P.s. R.S.V.P. is the abbreviation for the French phrase "répondez s'il vous plait" which means "Respond if you please"
  Reply within a few days by calling the phone number given on the invitation, or responding to the email address if provided.
- Do not accept the invitation if you do not honestly expect to attend.
- Never bring or ask to bring an uninvited guest.
- Call the day before (not an hour before the party) if you have any questions.
    Exception: if you will be more than 15-20 minutes late, call saying you were delayed (without going into detail) so they can start without you.
- When you respond, make your host aware of any dietary restrictions you have.
- Arrive on time. Never arrive earlier than the stated time.
- Pray for your host family the day of the event in order that the event might be a joy to them.
- Be sociable. A host or hostess will appreciate the guest who reaches out to other guests who are alone or do not know the others. Do not monopolize your host. Pay attention to people on both sides of you at a table.
- Respect your host's property. Wipe your shoes on the doormat if they are dirty. Remove your shoes if it is their custom.
- Apologize, but do not make a big issue of spilling or breaking something. Help clean up. If the item is valuable, try to replace.
- Leave the bathroom as clean as you found it.
- If it is necessary for you to leave early, do so quietly after you have thanked the host/ hostess. If you say good-byes to all the guests, it might tend to break up the party prematurely.

Hostess Gifts:

Show your appreciation for a meal with a small gift such as

· Flowers (especially appreciated by Europeans),
· Small plant
· Edibles (basket of fruit, chocolates, mints, coffees, teas, homemade food)
· Fancy paper guest towels
· Pretty tea towels
· Decorative candles
· Note cards
· Soaps and lotions
· A small Christian book, devotional or journal

Gift on the Way

· If you know where the local fruit and flower stands are, you might pick something up along the way.
· Forgot to plan ahead? Stop by a store and pick up a box of candy.
· Consider taking a gift for their children.

Gift Tip

Keep your eye out for hostess gifts on sale. Start a gift drawer or shelf. You will always have something on hand and won't have to stop on the way.

Thank You Notes:

Always remember to send a brief note of thanks within three days. Prompt is best, but "better late than never". I learned from my mother-in-law that you can never say thank you too much. People want to be appreciated and will "go to the moon" for you when you are gracious and appreciative. Keep thank you note cards on hand so you can write a thank you note as soon as you get home from attending an event.

A simple Thank You note should include comments on:
· your enjoyment of the event
· something about the event you found particularly memorable
· your appreciation of the invitation and desire to do it again

Thank you for the lovely evening in your beautiful home. The yummy food and warm fellowship will be a treasured memory for a long time

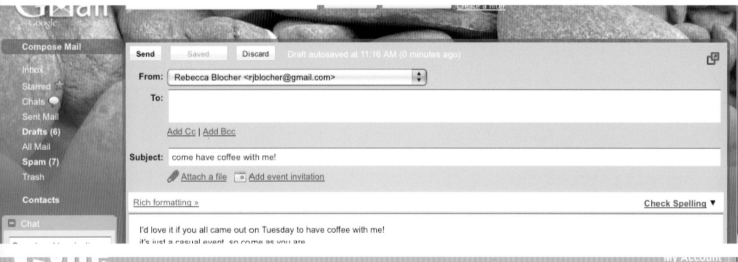

Compose Mail

Inbox
Starred
Chats
Sent Mail
Drafts (6)
All Mail
Spam (7)
Trash

Contacts

Chat

| Send | Saved | Discard | Draft autosaved at 11:16 AM (0 minutes ago) |

From: Rebecca Blocher <rjblocher@gmail.com>

To:

Add Cc | Add Bcc

Subject: come have coffee with me!

📎 Attach a file   Add event invitation

Rich formatting »   Check Spelling ▼

I'd love it if you all came out on Tuesday to have coffee with me!
it's just a casual event, so come as you are

HOME   INVITATIONS   ENTERTAINING   BLOG   GIFTS   ECARDS   EVITE MOBILE   Search

My Account

Invitations

Invitations Home

GENERAL
Featured Designs
All Designs
Design Your Own

EVENT TYPES

Modern Dinner Party

Host: Sarah Anderson
Location: Springfield Park
500 Clearview Road
Hometown, CA
Telephone: 310-555-1234
When: August 16, 2008 at 2 PM

It's time for our annual spring get-together. Pack up the picnic basket and join us for some fun in the sun. Bring your blankets, Fisbees and whatever you'd like to drink. We'll supply the footballs, snacks, (chips, pretzels, and fruit), sandwiches and cookies and brownies for dessert. Don't forget to bring sunscreen, bug spray and a hat - it's suppose to be sunny and warm! And yes, Mike will be bringing his iPod, so get ready to rock out!

you're invited to a
DINNER PARTY

GUEST LIST
Who's coming? As of Monday June 23, 2:15PM

YOUR REPLY
Will you attend, Johan? not Johan?
◉ Yes   ○ No   ○ Maybe

Total guests

Invitations

Invitations set the tone for any event. It is the first impression you make on your guests. A good invitation makes them curious and often determines whether or not they will attend your event. It should say, "This is not to be missed!" and should send them scrambling to check their calendar. Let it reflect the theme of your event. Throw some confetti into the envelope! Decorate your envelopes with stickers, rubber stamp designs or colored ink. Use brightly colored envelopes that set the invitation apart from all the other mail in their box. Handwrite the addresses. Do a few each day so you are not overwhelmed. All these ideas set the tone and say, "Don't miss this!" Nothing conveys your message as thoughtfully as a handwritten invitation. This is the most personal, but it is only practical for small, intimate events.

Spontaneous Invitations

Do not let all these ideas scare you off from "spur-of-the-moment" events. Often these are the most intimate and readily attended. There's nothing like a personal phone call that says, "You are special and we'd love to spend some time with you." Be sure to keep a list of whom you've called. If you leave a message on their answering machine, request that your call be returned. If too much time passes and you have not heard, call them again. If a child answers the phone, do not count on the parent getting the message. Phone back.

One Saturday morning we ran into our neighbors as we were jogging. They were on their way out with their baby jogger and dog. Right there, on the "spur-of-the-moment," I invited them to come over for brunch. As they finished jogging, I scrambled eggs and whipped up some French toast. Not only was it a memorable occasion in their lives but, later that fall, the wife visited my Bible study. She now knows the Lord. The brunch invitation became an invitation to Christ for her.

Check out the web site www. Entertaining ForEternity.com and the Resource Page at the back of this book for more invitation ideas.

EASY: Buy preprinted invitations and fill in the blanks. Special order these from web sites or catalogues.

EASIER: Download from our web site and print on your own computer. Or photo copy one from this book.

EASIEST: Phone or email or use electronic invitations (Evites®) that can be found on the web. Evites are the least personal way to extend an invitation. They are often not received because they are filtered out by internet service providers and may be sent to "spam" files. Email addresses do change from time to time, or if someone doesn't recognize your email address, they may delete your invitation without even opening it! Use this method only if you are confident the problems won't exist.

Invitation Details:

Go over your invitation carefully to make sure you have not omitted something important. Have another person check it, too. Even the most beautiful or clever invitation is of little use if it leaves out essential information. Check out the downloadable invitations on my web site or Real Simple's web site. There are also other suggestions in the Web Resources on page 205.

When Should Invitations be Sent?

Lunch, Teas and Coffees	Few days to 2 weeks
Informal Dinner	Few days to 3 weeks
Formal Dinner	3 to 6 weeks
Showers, Birthdays and Anniversaries	3 to 6 weeks
Graduation parties	3 weeks
Thanksgiving Dinner	2 weeks to 2 months
Christmas Party	1 month

Computers Help You

- type up your guest list.
- print out response sheets for recording RSVP's at each phone.
- design your theme invitations.
- print up your place cards or name tags containing your theme.
- use colorful graphics or clip art for everything.
- print your envelopes with theme clip art and return address labels.
- be creative and let your imagination and your computer do the work.

R.S.V.P.

Using "Regrets Only" can be tricky. I prefer RSVP. I like to know exactly who is coming so I can plan accordingly for food, space, and name tags. If you have not heard from a guest after a reasonable amount of time, you can always make a friendly phone call to check. The invitation may have gotten lost in the mail, or people who have been traveling are overwhelmed with the piles of mail upon their return.

I have run into friends after an event and had them say to me, "Oh, I really wanted to come to that! How did I miss it?" or "Your invitation got lost on my desk or in a pile of mail." My heart usually sinks because a good time was missed by both of us. R.S.V.P.s will help you manage your guest list and will guide you as you prepare your beverages and food.

Date:

Write out the day of the week as well as the date.

Time:

Be sure to include the starting and ending time unless you want your guests to hang around forever!

Dress:

If there is a style of dress, include this in the invitation by being specific rather than merely saying "Casual" which means something different to different people.

R.S.V.P.

Include your telephone number or your email address as an alternate way for people to respond to the invitation.

Directions or Map

If people have never been to your house, be sure to include detailed directions that show the easiest route. With GPS systems and cell phones, directions are not as much as an issue as they used to be. However, you may want to print a simple, accurate map or directions on a card. Include the card with your invitation. This information can be stored in a document on your computer so it is always ready to be printed.

Parking:

Give some suggestions where your guests can park, especially if parking is scarce in your neighborhood.

All the sample invitations in this book can be copied either two or three on an 8.5x11 sheet of paper or you can download and print them from the website: www.EntertainingForEternity.com

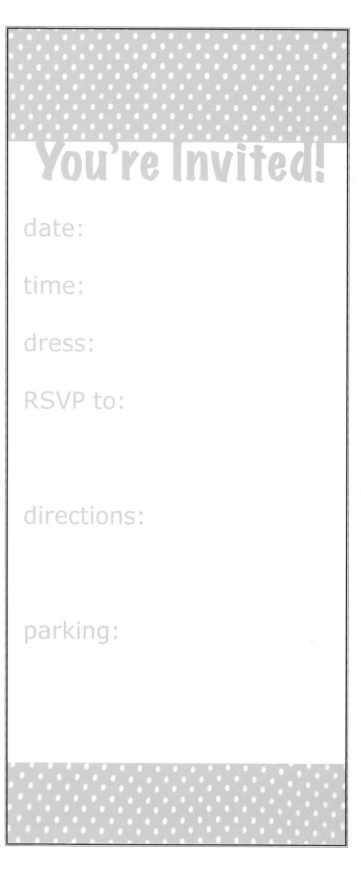

You're Invited!

date:

time:

dress:

RSVP to:

directions:

parking:

Chapter 3

Basic Types of Entertaining Events

Four basic types of events can be:

> Coffees or Teas
> Buffets and Dinners
> Large Events
> Overnight Guests

Some people are comfortable handling just a small group of people, and others have the attitude of "The more the merrier!" Do what you feel the Lord is leading you to do, but do not overcrowd your space. Remember to invite three times as many people as you would like to attend your event.

Estimating Sizes

- Sit-down Dinner: Between 6 to 10 works well around a table
- Buffet Supper: Between 10 to 15 (more if you have lap trays and seating)
- Potluck or Cookout: 15 or more depending on your seating
- Open House: This depends on room size and how many rooms you can use.
- Showers, Coffees & Teas: Between 10 to 15 (more if you have a large home)

Unexpected Guests:
Do not panic if an unexpected guest shows up. Quietly and quickly set another place and do not make him or her feel uncomfortable. Remember the definition of hospitality. No one will remember a slightly crowded table, but many will notice your graciousness in handling an awkward situation. The guest will feel welcomed and accepted rather than embarrassed.

If you are unsure about the amount of food available, wait until others have gone through the line. And, if someone asks why you aren't eating, explain that you have "kitchen privileges" and can eat later. It's more important that your guests feel the love of Christ and have their needs met. Sometime you may witness another "fish and loaves" miracle in your home! It's amazing how God seems to show up and make the food go farther.

If Things Go Wrong

- Take a deep breath
- Say a quick prayer
- Do not panic
- Be flexible
- Compromise
- Go to your emergency shelf

Coffees, Desserts and Teas

Coffees

Most Coffees are in the morning and are served with sweet breads and coffee cakes. A Tea can be held late morning or afternoon and includes light desserts. Basically Coffees and Desserts serve about the same things. Coffees can be held at anytime of day. Desserts are usually held in the evening, serving decaffeinated coffee or tea with pies, cookies or cakes.

Women tend to gather for morning coffee klatches, whereas Desserts can be for anyone. Both of these venues are great for showing heavenly hospitality. Evening Desserts for couples are especially good because men can enjoy them, too. (Be sure to check out the Winter section of this book for Christmas Coffee ideas.)

Here's a novel idea: Have a Sunday morning outreach Coffee. What better time is there to gather the un-churched than on a Sunday morning when they haven't anything else going on? Enlist the Sunday school classes to be praying during your outreach event in your neighborhood. Consequently, you have ready-made prayer teams assembled.

Coffees should include:

- Regular and decaffeinated coffee, various tea bags and hot water
- Pitcher of water or juice for people who don't drink coffee or tea
- Coffee cake or nut breads
- Plate of fresh fruit for those watching their weight

Creamer Tip

Put a dab of butter under the lip of your creamer. It will keep it from dripping.

Desserts

These should be much the same as coffees except substituting dessert food for coffee cakes and breads.

Suggested menu items:

- Pie
- Cake
- Dessert Jell-O®
- Bavarian Creams
- Mousse*
- Petit Fours
- Brownies cut into small pieces*
- Cookies*
- Cut up fruit*

(*for those who want fewer calories.)

Teas

There's nothing quite as soothing as sipping a hot cup of tea. Tea conjures up memories of Alice in Wonderland or Peter Rabbit's chamomile tea before being put to bed. A simple Afternoon Tea has the advantage of being able to be prepared well in advance. Only a pot of water needs to be boiled as the guests arrive. The whistle of the tea kettle is part of the Tea party atmosphere. There's something very pleasant about the sound of tea spoons being stirred in dainty tea cups. Always keep a package of special cookies in your pantry for spur-of-the-moment Teas.

Teas are an easy way to show hospitality. Tea rooms are springing up all over the country and ladies are digging out their grandmother's tea cup collections from the attic. Bakeries and gourmet grocery stores are offering all sorts of delightful items that can be picked up on the way home from running errands.

I have a pastor friend and his wife who have "tea time" every afternoon together. It's their debriefing time without the children. They sip their tea quietly in the living room before the dinner rush and catch up on their activities. The children are instructed to busy themselves with homework or chores in another part of the house so their parents can spend uninterrupted time together.

One of my fondest childhood memories is going to Tea with my mother and sister at Sibley's Tea Room in Rochester, New York. We would order tea and cinnamon toast cut in dainty triangles. We would then watch as models walked between the tables displaying the latest fashions from the department store. Many little girls were given a tea set at one time or another. Dolls and teddy bears were lined up and served. I still remember the tiny tea set my parents bought for me one time on a trip to my grandmother's house. Why not capitalize on every woman's warm fuzzy memories and use tea to share the gospel? I've done it in many venues. One church reached out to the mothers of the children who came to their Daily Vacation Bible School (DVBS). After the children were settled in their classes, the moms were loaded up in vans and driven to a private tea room.

When the ladies arrived, they discovered racks of all sorts of hats to try on in front of a huge mirror. After many laughs, each woman chose the perfect hat to complete her outfit. The women found their places at tables for two or four all around the room. Each table was set with different china. As the women were chatting, the hostess's retired husband, wearing a tuxedo, came out carrying tiered tea plates for each table. When they were almost finished eating, the pastor's wife introduced me and I shared a "tea story". The whole event was a welcome change from the usual children's program that most churches put on at the end of Bible School.

Another church asked me to speak at their annual Mother-Daughter Tea. When I arrived early, the ladies were busy setting up their

"If you are cold, tea will warm you,
If you are heated, it will cool you,
If you are depressed, it will cheer you,
If you are excited, it will calm you."
- William E. Gladstone (1809-1898)

Tea Handouts

Go to the website at www.EntertainingFor Eternity.com for "tea-isms" that you can print and place at each person's place at the table.

individual tea tables with china from their own homes. Each table had two hostesses who were responsible for decorating and for furnishing the "crumpets" for their table. The table hostesses invited eight friends who did not know the Lord.

What fun it was for me to walk around and see each table with its own style and personality. Some had romantic Victorian china. Some had Lenox. Some had Royal Doulton. Some were more casual place settings. Each table had its own tea pot as well. There were centerpieces of roses, daisies, or hydrangeas. Some had lace and some had chintz tablecloths. Everything was brought from home so that the only thing that had to be done in the kitchen was to boil water for the teapots.

As I was walking around admiring the different tea pots, I noticed one with a verse on it and wondered out loud what it meant. Suddenly from behind me I heard a woman exclaim in a deep British accent, "Oh, that's the song we used to sing back in England every day at school before going home for lunch." I asked her if she knew the tune, and next thing we knew the pianist and the British lady were entertaining us.

Then the British woman explained in her charming British accent, how to fix a "proper pot of tea". She said that you first must warm the pot by sloshing boiled water around in it. Then tea is only made with boiling water and must steep for at least 3 - 5 minutes. The table hostesses then filed in with their tea pots and the lovely afternoon began.

The mood in the room was light and full of laughter and chatter, so that by the time I was introduced, almost any un-churched woman

was ready to hear the Gospel. Many came to a saving knowledge of Christ that afternoon.

Each invited guest seemed to be so glad she had come. More unbelievers came to this event than may have gone on their own to a regular Sunday morning church service. There were several teenage girls from the youth group who brought their moms. Many of these moms didn't attend the church at all. A nice thing about a Tea is that it doesn't have to be for a large crowd. You can put a "three hour log" in your fireplace and simply invited a friend for tea and cookies. Sitting on the couch in front of a warm fire on a cold afternoon is a pleasant experience and a special time for conversation. Be sensitive to the special needs and concerns of your neighbors. One day my German neighbor phoned to say that her father-in-law had died back in Germany. That afternoon over a cup of tea at my kitchen table I was able to give her hope and share Christ with her. She hugged and thanked me profusely as she left.

Teas can be organized well ahead of time. I once put on a Tea to honor my friend, Vonette Bright and wanted to invite Campus Crusade staff members who lived in the area. However, I was involved in a conference all week long, staying at a local hotel. So, I set the table the weekend before, prepared the goodies, and froze them. Other goodies I picked up at the store on the way home. I enlisted the help of several friends to run the kitchen and bring sandwiches. The mood was festive as some of my friends put the finishing touches on the trays of food. I was relaxed because most of the work had been done ahead of time. That's the key to larger events; do as much as you can ahead of time.

Tea Tips

-Use fresh water
-Warm the teapot
with hot water
-Pour boiling
water over loose
tea or bags
-Steep the tea for
3 to 5 minutes; no
longer.
-Remove the bags
so the tea will not
get too strong

More recently I hosted a Tea for governors' wives while they were in Washington, D.C. for meetings. I enlisted the help of a girlfriend who does catering which freed me to greet the ladies and be the speaker at the event which was held on a snowy afternoon at the Folgers Shakespeare Library behind the Capitol. The Tudor-style room with its carved paneling and beams, antique furniture and stone fireplaces provided the atmosphere of having tea in Shakespearean England. As the ladies came in from an afternoon of formal seminars and meetings and saw the teapots, roses and crumpets, we heard them sigh, "Ahhh!" After tea was poured, the ladies sat around and visited happily and sipped tea as I spoke.

Whether you're serving a crowd or a neighbor at the kitchen table, there's just something about tea that leaves a warm, comforting memory. It's a perfect way to share your faith.

Your speaker may wish to use the talks in this manual. Use some of the conversation simulators in this book or have the ladies answer the following questions as you pour tea and relax:

1. Why has tea had such a big resurgence in America?

2. What is your favorite "tea memory"?

You might want to use the quotes from Emilie Barnes' book, Everything I Know I Learned Over Tea, which are given at the end of this section. These can be cut apart and put at different places at your table or passed around to your guests as they sit in your family room. The quotes can be reproduced on decorative paper, or use tea-themed rubber stamps to decorate your own paper.

A marvelous web site where you can find Tea ideas is: www.teaforallreasons.com. This is maintained by my friend Marsha Richards who gives Tea seminars and has a beautiful and extensive collection of tea cups and teapots. You will find everything you need at this web site to put on a perfect Tea.

Two Types of Teas

Basically, Teas fall into two categories:

- Basic afternoon Tea served 2:00- 4:00pm
- High Tea served like a light supper at 5:00- 7:00pm

A Simple Tea Menu

Fancy cookies

Scones with clotted cream or jam

Egg salad sandwiches cut in cute shapes

Open faced cream cheese sandwiches with sliced cucumbers on top

Strawberries and grapes

Most all of these menu items can be bought already prepared at the local grocery store. The sandwiches can be labor intensive but do not have to be. Most of the time I just serve fancy cookies and sliced fruit. Keep Pepperidge Farm cookies or other fancy cookies on hand so you'll be prepared when friends drop by for a "spot of tea" on a moment's notice.

Menu Suggestions

- **Cinnamon toast**
  (Children love it and they are great for a quick "tea for two".)
- **Tea Sandwiches**
  (Tiny finger sandwiches for Low Tea and hearty full ones for High Tea.)
- **Chocolate-dipped strawberries**
- **Cookies, scones with jam and clotted cream**
- **A variety of teas** (let your guests choose)
- **Lemons and milk** (never cream)
- **Sugar cubes** (fun but not necessary)

Tip

Tea Sandwiches (can be made ahead of time and kept fresh in the refrigerator by covering them with damp paper towels, tea towels or lettuce leaves.)

Proper way to eat scones

Cut scones in half like a hamburger bun and place jam on both halves topped by the cream. Do not put the halves back together.

Tea Apron

Buy a white apron from the craft store and stencil tea cups on it with craft paints. Your "pouring friend" will feel very special.

Serving Suggestions

You do not need a fancy silver tea service. A simple pot will do. If six or more are coming, ask a friend to pour and attend to the kettle and pot so that you are free to chat with your guests. It is an honor to be asked to pour tea.

Buffets and Dinner Parties

"They broke bread in their homes and
ate together with glad and sincere hearts,
praising God and enjoying the favor of all the people."
Acts 2:46b-47 NIV

Dinners can be served family-style, restaurant-style or buffet-style depending on the size of your group, the layout of your home or the formality of your event. Generally use family-style for small gatherings, and buffet-style for larger groups. You may also fill plates in the kitchen. For formal dinners (restaurant-style), you may wish to fill plates with food in the kitchen and serve your guests seated at the dining room table. At family-style dinners, platters of food are passed and guests serve themselves. This is more informal, and easily lends itself to "heavenly hospitality." Dining buffet-style, guests serve themselves from the food table and sit elsewhere to eat. You may choose to gather people together for prayer, and then give them instructions on getting their food.

Buffet Meals

The beauty of a buffet is that almost everything can be done in advance. The entire buffet table can be set and ready to go. If you are providing all the food, you can have it ready in the refrigerator. Main dish casseroles can be kept warm in the oven or on warming trays.

You can use a buffet table for serving:

- A sit-down meal at one large table
- A large crowd at multiple tables
- Guests seated in chairs around your living room or family room.

Buffet table tips

- Always begin your buffet table line with plates and napkins and end with silverware.
- When the buffet table is against the wall, place table decorations against the wall and the food around the perimeter. Consider grouping cold and hot dishes.
- When the buffet table is in the center of the room, keep any decor to the center of the table and keep the service at the enter/exit side of the room.
- For a large crowd, duplicate service on either end of the table.

 for diagrams and examples of buffet table layouts see www.EntertainingForEternity.com

Buffet Table

A long table (5 feet) or several small tables, a dining room side board or even a kitchen counter can provide for your buffet table. Remember to plan carefully where you are going to place each serving dish of food.

If you can arrange your buffet so people can serve themselves from both sides, the lines will go quicker. Place two serving spoons in each dish or have duplicate dishes of food on both sides of the table. Try creating different heights by hiding small, sturdy boxes under the tablecloth. This will not only make your table look interesting, but it will make it easier for guests to reach other platters or dishes. Scatter some fresh flowers, ivy or greenery on your table to create color.

Your room layout and the amount of available space will determine whether you can have two serving lines. Consider your flow so that you do not create a "traffic jam."

Plan Traffic Routes

- Make sure guests can move easily around the buffet table.
- Place a buffet table against the wall or use a side board for small crowds.
- Arrange the food in logical order: plates, salad, vegetables, meat or main dish followed by bread or rolls with relishes or toppings at the end.
- Try to serve salads or dishes that only require one utensil to pick up the food allowing the guest's other hand to hold the plate.
- Place the silverware on the tables or on trays or tie them up in the napkin in such a way that they can be picked up at the end.
- Use twin setups for a crowd so there can be two serving lines with the table pulled away from the wall.
- Clear the main course before setting out the dessert buffet on the same table. If you are able to have a separate dessert buffet, do it in another location.

Beverage Stations

It's usually best to have your drinks at a station away from your food buffet. Guests can get their beverages after their plates are filled. Serving drinks at the buffet table means that they would have one more item to juggle. You might wish to have the table already set with glasses of ice water.

Cold Drinks

Set up a cold drink station, which may include pitchers of ice water or ice tea, an ice bucket or bowl of ice. Limiting the selections makes it easier and less expensive. You might want to serve liters of soft drinks or pitchers of lemonade or juice. Put out the beverage glasses you intend for them to use. For large picnic-style events use plastic disposable cups and provide a marker for guests to put their names on their cups. For some events, you might want to use a punch bowl with punch cups.

Hot Drinks

A hot drink station can be near the coffee maker or the desserts. In addition to your coffee maker, have thermoses of hot water next to a variety of tea bags or hot drink mixes. Provide sugar, sugar substitute and creamer near the hot drinks. (For sit-down dinners, you may want to have your sugar and creamer on a tiny tray to pass around the table or walk with. The little tray makes it easier to pass and keep the sugars and cream together. It also catches the drip off the creamer and saves your table cloth.)

Silverware

I usually put silverware in a basket along with the napkins at the end of the buffet table. When guests finally have a free hand, it won't be so awkward. The most convenient manner is to tie the silverware together to the napkin with a ribbon. Most of the time all they need is a fork. Another idea is to have silverware caddies with the utensils in them and the napkins in a neat pile near those. Again, if they are going through the line and sitting at already set tables you eliminate these problems.

Paper Plates and Plasticware

For large outdoor picnics, consider using heavy-duty plastic, Styrofoam®, or paper plates and sturdy plastic knives and forks.

Guest Seating

If you are not using a dining table to seat your guests, make sure you have ample seating for the number of people attending your meal. You can use several rooms and even put your dining room chairs around the rooms intermingled with your couches and upholstered furniture. That will free up your dining table to serve as your buffet table.

However, if guests are sitting around the room away from the table, make sure your plates are sturdy, or use lap trays. It's best to have small side tables or coffee tables for beverages. Set out coasters to protect your furniture from having moisture rings. If your guests are not eating at tables, limit the knick-knacks on side tables and coffee table so guests will have places to set their drinks down.

When guests do not know each other, you might want to control the seating and use place cards and tables to make sure there's a congenial mix of personalities and interests. Be sensitive to shy people who remain by themselves. Introduce them to others and encourage them to join in other groups.

Special Considerations for Buffets

- Do not crowd your buffet table. Decorate your buffet with greenery, flowers and candles. Place flowers or sprinkle confetti on the table between the platters. Place candles in the center of the table, away from guests' sleeves!
- Separate drink and dessert stations from buffets.
- Tie napkins around silverware using colorful ribbon to make it easier for guests to pick them up.
- Choose meals that fit easily on a person's plate.
- Choose food items that can be served with one hand, remembering that your guests' other hand will be holding their dinner plates. If available, allow space for guests to set down their plates while serving.
- Cut meats and casseroles into serving size pieces. It's easiest if food is already cut into bite-sized portions requiring only a fork. Spoons can be laid out at the coffee station.
- Serve rolls or pre-sliced bread. If guests are not going to a dining table where butter dishes will be available, then the bread will have to be buttered. (Nothing holds a line up more than waiting for people to spread butter or mayonnaise)
- Keep warm dishes warm and cold dishes cold. Use warming trays or casseroles or chaffing dishes with candles. In hot weather place items like gelatin salads or mayonnaise salads over a larger dish of ice.
- Keep the buffet table stocked. Keep an eye on your buffet table so as not to run out of an item. After everyone is through the line, restock it with whatever you have left in the kitchen and then sit down and enjoy your meal with your guests.
- Encourage guests not to wait for you, the hostess, before they start eating. That will allow you to restock the buffet before guests are ready for second helpings.

Buffet Tray Tip

Buy inexpensive bamboo trays at home goods stores.
If you get several friends to go in with you and each buys some, you can share with each other when you have large crowds.

Menu Planning for Dinners or Buffets

Whether it is a meal, a Tea or a Dessert, write out your menu and line up all the recipe cards you will use. Make a list of ingredients you may need to buy and put that list in your purse. Remember to plan only foods that you've tried before and know are good. Experimenting with recipes will only add drama to your day. Serve food that can be made well in advance. If you are rushing around in the kitchen when guests arrive, it will make them feel like they are an inconvenience to you.

Put a neat copy of your menu on your refrigerator door or counter and check it as you take the food to the table or buffet. That way you will not forget the salad in the back of the refrigerator or the rolls in the pantry. Nothing is more disconcerting than discovering at the end of the event that something was forgotten.

Create a time chart of how long each menu item will take to prepare. It's almost an art to have everything done at the same time. Plan your oven use by considering times and temperatures.

Considerations for a Buffet Menu

The menu content can be much like a dinner except your guests serve themselves from dishes on a side board or buffet table. Remember to prepare extra food if guests will fill their own plates.

- Consider keeping the food warm in chafing dishes, on warming trays or in dishes that have small candles under them.
- Make sure your bowl or platter is big enough so that you will not have to replenish it before all your guests go through the line.
- Consider using salad plates so that gelatin or frozen salads won't have to go on the same plate as hot food.

Menu should include

- Hors d'oeuvres ("Finger food" which can be eaten in 1-2 bites)
- Main Dish Casserole with meat and vegetables
- Meat, Chicken or Fish (protein source)
- Vegetables
- Starch (potatoes, rice or pasta)
- Salad
- Bread or rolls & butter
- Dessert

Rice Cooker Idea

Buy a rice cooker and you'll always have perfect rice ready ahead of time and kept warm.

Menu Planning

- Consider the age of your guests. If children are invited, you may wish to include "kid-friendly" food.
- Use foods that are in season. They'll taste better and be cheaper. Many people are health conscious so serve nutritious, healthy food.
- Serve only things that you have tried before. Do not try new things out on guests. Practice on your husband or family first to prevent last minute disasters. Develop a personal repertoire or group of menus that you are comfortable with and have been successful with in the past. Write these on cards for future use to prevent serving the same thing to the same group of people.
- Take the main meal into account when selecting the dessert. Serve something light if you have prepared a heavy meal.
- Plan oven use wisely.
  - Consider the space that will be needed.
  - Note different oven temperatures needed.

- Remember to vary the flavors, colors and textures of your foods.
  Chicken, white rice, cauliflower, and pineapple and banana salad with white rolls could look pretty bland and unappetizing. Avoid foods that clash, such as beets, tomatoes and radishes.
- Consider textures and repetition.
  - When there's a cheese topping, do not use cheese in another dish.
  - Have cream sauce in only one dish.
  - This does not apply to serving a fruit salad and fruit dessert! They could be completely different and be just fine – fruit salad and apple pie for example!

Dietary Restrictions

Be sensitive to dietary needs your guest may have, especially if they are vegetarians. Try to find out ahead of time if your guests have any allergies or particular restrictions. Include some food items that they may enjoy and avoid calling attention to the issue. Keep your menus simple, not exotic and you shouldn't run into very many problems.

Presentation

Table and food presentation sets the tone and gives the first impression. It is said, "The eyes taste it first." A sprig of parsley, fresh mint or fruit will add welcome color.

Planning Tip

Write out the exact times of the day that each dish goes in the oven. For example:
- 4:30 Pre-heat oven
- 4:45 Put roast in at 350°
- 5:30 Potato casserole
- 6:15 Warm up bread
- 6:30 Serve

Buffet or Dinner Tip

People often feel more involved if you have them bring part of the meal. It makes the event more affordable and the preparation easier. A bonus is you have more time with your guests and will be able to entertain more often with less stress. The downside is you have to be prepared if someone forgets their item or does not bring enough for the whole crowd.

Calculating amounts of food per person

Meats	1/4 pound for each person
Vegetables	1/2 Cup per serving
Potatoes	3/4 Cup per serving
Rice	½ Cup cooked rice
Tossed Salad	1 1/2 Cup
Rolls	1 per person. Men eat more; women less, so it will balance out
Desserts:	8" Cake serves 8 people
	9" Cake serves 8 – 10 people
	10" Cake serves 10 – 12 people
	9" X 13" Cake serves 12 people
	8" Pie serves 8 people
	9" Pie serves 8-10 people
	10" Pie serves 10 -12 people
	Cookie or Bars: Allow 2 - 3 per person

Menu Planning Sheet

Appetizers: _____

_____

_____

Main Dish: _____

Vegetables: _____

Starch: _____

Salad: _____

Bread: _____

Dessert: _____

Beverages: _____

Trays

Cheese board & knives

Dip dishes

Cracker baskets or trays

Platter or chafing dish

Vegetable bowls

Serving spoons & forks

Large salad bowl

Individual salad bowls

Bread roll basket

Bread plates

Cake pedestal or trays

Dessert plates

Punch cups

Goblets or glasses

Nametags

Cocktail napkins

Table flatware

Placecards

Votives & Candles

Table Decorations

All sorts of items can be placed on a tablecloth to add color or interest. Pick items that are connected to your theme or use what you have available to you and what is in season:

- Ivy from your yard
- Christmas greenery with pine cones or Christmas ornaments
- Confetti
- Dried or fresh cut flowers such as pansies
- Streamers or wired ribbon curled down the table
- Table runners
- Votive candles (try them on mirrors or mix them in with the other items)

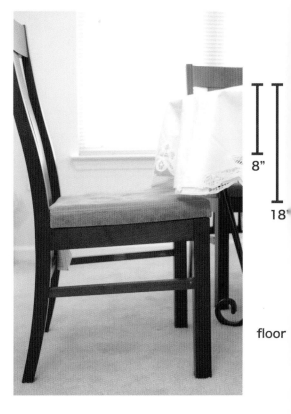

Table Linens

Coordinate the color and theme to make your table special. Placemats are usually less formal than table cloths. Table cloths can be bought on sale or at discount stores. Look for bargains at "after-holiday sales". Stores like JC Penney often have tablecloths on sale in any size for $20. Banquet size cloths fit 4x8 plywood table tops. Buy 3 yards of 60" wide fabric at the yard goods store. Flannel-backed vinyl tablecloths can be used for children or for outdoor picnics. The table cloth should not be so long that it rests on guests' laps. Put a foam-backed table pad under your table cloth to protect your table and silence the clatter of dishes on the table. These can be purchased at fabric stores by the yard. They do not need to be fancy.

Table "runners" or "square toppers" can be a great way to spice up a plain cloth and bring your theme in without having to buy

different cloths for each holiday or theme. Try table squares on top of a plain cloth. Place a square on the diagonal over another full size cloth. Purchase squares of holiday-designed fabric. Cut the edges with pinking sheers or sew narrow hems on them. Put these on top of a plain white full size table cloth. It's a nice way to add seasonal color without having to buy full-size tablecloths.

Unused bed sheets make good table cloths for big tables. A king-size sheet will make a floor-length cloth for a 48 inch round table (standard rental table size).

Store your tablecloths folded on hangers in a closet. Dry cleaners often have extra thick table cloth hangers. Label each hanger with the dimensions of the tablecloth.

Children's Linen Tip

Buy some clear plastic at the fabric store and cut into large place mat sizes for the places children will be sitting. This will protect your tablecloth from getting stained.

Table Cloth Drop

· Best is 18"
· 8" for less formal occasions.
· To the floor only for buffet tables

Table Cloth Colors

White or off White: for dressy occasions
Red: for Christmas, Valentine's Day, Patriotic
     events
Green: for Fall, St. Patrick's Day, or Christmas
Red Checked: for cookouts or Italian food
Pastel: for spring occasions or showers

Napkins

Napkins can be paper or cloth and can be a way to add color to your table. If you have a white table cloth, try brightly colored napkins that match the colors of your centerpiece or dishes. Obviously paper napkins are less expensive than cloth napkins, but also watch for discount store sales on cloth napkins. Dollar store bandanas can be used for napkins and add a festive touch to cookouts and Texas barbeques.

Napkin Rings

can be as simple as wired ribbon or raffia tied around gathered napkins or wooden drapery rings with a bow tied on the ring. These can be personalized using paint pens or markers and given to your guests as party favors. You may wish to start a collection of napkin rings to be used for special occasions or holidays.

Folding Napkins

Setting a beautiful table, like serving good food, tells family and friends they are special! Napkins may be placed at the left of the forks or under the forks, with open corners at lower right. They can also be folded and placed on the dinner plate or arranged in the glass.

Decorating Tip

Ribbon that has been re-enforced with wire on the edges works great for many projects and always holds its shape. It can easily be re-used for many projects.

Some clever and beautiful ways to fold napkins are on the companion web site to this book www. EntertainingFor Eternity.com

Candles

Candles always add ambiance and make an event seem special. Watch out for inexpensive ones that tend to drip. Votives lined down the center of the table twinkle and add to the festive feel. These can be placed on the table along with tall tapers in the center of the table. Try candles of different height and diameter or use tapers in a grouping. Putting candles on a mirror reflects the light and adds more sparkle to your table. Small 12" mirrors can be bought at most craft stores.

Candle Wax Warnings

Assign a responsible person to extinguish your candles using with a snuffer.
Blow candles out by cupping your hand behind the flame.
Do not blow too hard!
Never pick up and attempt to move a candle with melted wax. (Wait until the wax solidifies.)

Oops! Wax on the Tablecloth

· Wait until the wax is solidified.
· Chill with an ice cube.
· Scrape off as much as you can with a dull butter knife.
· Stretch the waxed part of the cloth over a strainer in a sink with the wax side down.
· Pour boiling water slowly over the waxed area until you think it's all melted away.
· Spot treat with detergent or pre-wash product before you launder.

Decoration Stash

-All sorts of candles
-Balloons
-Crepe paper rolls
-Special occasion napkins
-Rolls of wired ribbon
-Index cards & markers

Centerpieces

Quite often the first thing that comes to mind when thinking of a centerpiece is a floral arrangement. These can be costly or require a talent you may not have. Check your yard to see what is available. It may surprise you. There's nothing wrong with dried arrangements during the winter or a couple of random daffodils in a bud vase. Most grocery stores have some inexpensive flowers like mums or carnations. If it's a special occasion, a cake may be all you need in the center of the table. You could also fill a glass pedestal bowl with fresh fruit, some seasonal items, or something that goes with your theme. Make sure your centerpiece is not too tall. Guests should be able to see over it easily to make conversation across the table. Tie it into your theme or the season of the year.

Ideas

{1} **Valentines:** Place red & white carnations in a vase with a red ribbon around it. Scatter red paper hearts all over a white tablecloth.

{2} **Spring:** Choose several small pots of spring flowers (hyacinth, tulips, small daffodils, crocuses, primrose) in a large basket and place sphagnum moss or Easter grass around the pots. Tie a colorful wired ribbon bow on the basket and use more of the same ribbon to tie around the napkins. (You can plant the flowers in your yard afterwards.)

{3} **Picnic Tables:** Set small pots of white mums on a red-checked tablecloth. Stencil stars on the pots.

{4} **Barbeque:** Use cowboy hat and bandana

{5} **Bridal Shower or Engagement Party:** Select several 5x7" frames with the couple's photos in them. Sprinkle craft store plastic wedding rings around the table. Add a bud vase of roses and sprinkle rose petals around the table. Red roses indicate "love."

{6} **Baby Shower:** Cut a watermelon in the shape of a baby carriage. Make wheels for the carriage using orange slices and secure them with tooth picks. Fill the "carriage" with fruit salad. Use pink carnations for a baby girl and blue carnations for a baby boy.

{7} **Fall:** Choose a small hollowed pumpkin or cut off the top of an artificial pumpkin and fill it with mums or dried flowers. Sprinkle fall leaves on the table. Fill a large Mason jar with candy corn and insert fall silk flowers in it.

{8} **Thanksgiving:** Buy a craft store cornucopia and have fresh fruit or vegetables tumbling out.

{9} **Christmas:** Select red and white carnations with holly or evergreens and pine cones from the woods. For glitz spray paint the holly and cones either silver or gold and place them on the table. Gift wrap several small boxes with the same paper and wired ribbon bows. Stack them in a grouping together. Add spirals of the same ribbon down the center of the table and tie the napkins with the ribbon.

{10} **New Years:** Set a large clock set at 12 o'clock midnight and have curls of confetti-like streamers cascading down and around it on the table. Sprinkle more confetti around the table.

{2}

{3}

{4}

{7}

{5}

{8}

{6}

{10}

Dishes

Your dishes do not need to be either fancy or expensive to set a pretty table. People will remember the laughter around your table a lot longer than impressive china. White dishes are versatile and interchangeable and look nice with any tablecloth, color scheme or holiday decor. They also work well with colorful, busy patterned tablecloths. A red tablecloth and white dishes looks great for both Christmas and Valentines Day. Red-checked cloth and white dishes are grand for Italian themes or cookouts. Against a dark green tablecloth, you can decorate for Christmas, St. Patrick's Day, or for a fall theme with fall leaves strewn about the table and a pumpkin centerpiece. Spice up your table with colorful accent serving pieces or your centerpiece.

The Place Setting

This diagram shows a very formal setting. Naturally, you adjust the setting according to what's on your menu and type of occasion. The plate, glass and basic silverware stay the same for any meal.

bread plate

butter knife

dessert spoon

dessert fork

cup / goblet

dinner plate

salad fork

dinnner fork

dinner knife

teaspoon

soup spoon

Details to Consider

- Allow about 24 inches for each place setting, and put each plate an inch from the table edge. If placemats are used, they should come to the edge of the table.
- Place silverware "Outside-in": spoons, forks, knives are placed in the order in which they will be used, starting with the pieces farthest from the dinner plate.
- Place knife and spoons to the right of the plate, the forks to the left.
- Put cutting edge of knife toward the plate.
- Set water glass or goblet just above the tip of the knife blade.
- Place cup and saucer to the right of the glass.
- Fold napkins in squares, triangles or oblong shapes. They can be placed to the left of the forks, under the forks, or placd on the dinner plates.
- Serve the dessert utensil with the dessert.

Meal Time Prayer

Saying a prayer before dinner is a perfect time to give a hint of your family's spiritual side. My husband always says something like, "It's our custom at our house to say grace before we eat." He pauses and then says a simple "Thanks" for the food and for the event that we've gathered for. He does this in everyday simple language and keeps it brief. Remarkable conversations often ensue with our guests who do not know the Lord. It's amazing how powerful something so simple can be!

For families that are musical, try singing the Doxology as your blessing, or use the meal time blessing printed below. Almost everyone knows the song, Edelweiss, from the famous movie, The Sound of Music. If you have a piano or guitar, it's even better. Singing something like this is fun and enjoyable. Look around your table, everyone will be smiling!

Easy Table Grace
(Sung to the tune of Edelweiss)

Bless our friends, Bless our food
Come Lord Jesus, sit with us.
May our talk grow with peace.
May your love surround us.
Friendship and love may it
bloom and grow,
bloom and grow forever.
Bless our friends, Bless our food.
Come, O Lord and sit with us.

Sit-Down Meals

Sit-down meals can be informal, family-style meals or more formal meals where a guest is served a plate of food by the host or hostess. Plates are served and cleared from the left, while beverages are served and cleared from the right. In family-style meals, the food is on the table in bowls or on platters which are passed counter-clockwise around the table, starting with the guest of honor. Serving dishes are received from the left and then passed on to the right. This frees up the right hand to serve oneself. (Most people are right handed.)

Seating Your Guests

Place cards help you with the seating arrangement at your table. Consider ahead of time how you will seat your guests to make sure the conversation will flow well.

- You and your spouse, or co-host should sit at opposite ends of the table.
- Couples and close friends should sit apart from each other in order to meet someone new.
- Men and women, traditionally, should sit in alternating chairs.
- Strong conversationalists should be spread around.
- Left handed people should be seated at the left end corners.
- Guests of honor at formal events: female honored guest sits next to male host and male honored guest sits next to female hostess.

By using place cards, you can group people with similar interests, backgrounds, or professions at the same table.

copy this page
and use it to plan!

Dinner Party Checklist

Purpose identified: Fellowship, Relational or Invitational

Theme selected: _____

Event type chosen: _____

Date chosen: _____

Time chosen: _____

☐ Guest list made

☐ Invitation made

☐ Invitations sent

☐ Menu planned

☐ Shopping list made

☐ Cooking schedule written down

☐ Serving dishes washed and laid out with serving flatware/utensils

☐ Tablecloth washed and ironed

☐ Dishes and silverware counted and clean

Chapter 4

Eternal Etiquette - Pleasing Pleasantries

In the New Testament, Paul admonishes us to "be all things to all men in order that we might win some." He means that we should not be a "stumbling block" to distract or keep people from coming to Christ. This is what "Pleasing Pleasantries" is all about. Good manners, for the Christian, mean looking out for the interests and comfort of others. As Christians, we reflect Christ. When people come into our home, we do not want anything to distract them from the love of Christ.

The Lord taught us that we should think of others as more important than ourselves. (Romans 15:2; Philippians 2:3) That's what "eternal etiquette" is all about. It should permeate every part of our lives and everything we do. It's the "golden rule" applied to every area of life, whether someone surprises us at our front door, shares a meal or spends the night. (The house guest section will also deal with some of the "eternal etiquette" we need to remember).

Pleasing Table Manners

No matter how casual our culture has become, the importance of etiquette still remains. The real purpose of table manners in the beginning was to make the dining experience more pleasant. If we are confident in our own manners, we can focus on the people around us-- whether it is a job interview, a formal meal or dinner with the President of the United States.

Through our ministry in Washington D.C., our children have dined with Ambassadors, Senators and Congressmen. We seldom had to worry about our kids but instead could focus on ministering to those at our table. Now that the children are grown, they are relaxed and do not have to think about whether or not they are doing the "right thing".

Good manners make us more pleasant to be around. No one enjoys dining with a person who chews with an open mouth or leans on the table shoveling in food with their head down. We are judged by our table manners and we, unconsciously, judge others by theirs. One evening after an international guest left, our children made sure we knew that the man had "smacked" his lips as he ate. (In his culture this was acceptable and indicated that the meal was good.) Culturally appropriate manners are proper in any setting.

> "Even if we believe that it makes no difference to the Lord whether we do these things, still we cannot just go ahead and do them to please ourselves; for we must bear the burden of being considerate...of others."
> Romans 15:1-2 LB

The information in this section will take you through some of the elements of dining etiquette. If you want to learn more about formal events check out a marvelous little book called, The Little Book of Etiquette from the Protocol School of Washington can be ordered from Amazon.com

Fortunately, the rules of dining etiquette are straightforward and easy to master. You may need to unlearn some bad habits so that you can begin to set a good example of "heavenly hospitality". Most of all, you will be better able to focus on the people around you and to share the love of Jesus Christ.

At the Table

Getting Seated

If you are out at a dinner party, make sure to greet each person sometime before you are called to the dinner table. Introduce yourself to those you did not meet beforehand. Greet guests you already know by name.

Stand behind your chair until the hostess has been seated. To seat yourself, or to be seated by someone, sit down from the right side of your chair. Gentlemen still pull out chairs for women and they still rise when a lady approaches their table. This courtesy should be acknowledged with a gracious "Thank you".

Once you are seated, take a look at the place setting carefully. A simple rule of thumb is to use the silverware from the outside and move toward the plate. Generally, the outside or smaller fork is for the salad and the larger fork is used for the dinner. If there are two spoons, the larger one, or outside one is probably for the soup. Silverware placed above the plate is for dessert.

Napkins

When the host or hostess picks up his or her napkin, you may then put yours on your lap. Keep your napkin folded in half, placing the fold toward your waist. Smaller luncheon napkins are opened fully on your lap.

- Wipe your fingers and blot your mouth frequently with your napkin.
- Never lick your fingers
- Blot your lipstick before coming to the table so as not to stain napkins.
- Do not "mop" your face with your napkin; only blot your mouth.
- Never dip your napkin in a water glass to wipe a stain. Excuse yourself to the restroom to check a stain.
- If you must leave the table for any reason, place your napkin on the chair seat and slide your chair under the table as you leave.

Leave your napkin in your lap until the host signals the end of the meal by putting his or her napkin to the left of his plate. Do not re-fold your napkin. Pick it up from the center and place it loosely on the table to the left of your plate. Never put it on the soiled plate.

Glassware and Plates

Bread plates are placed on the left side of the plate, above the forks. If the person on your left mistakenly uses your bread plate, which often happens, use your dinner plate for bread and don't call attention to the mistake. Resist the urge to take the bread plate on your right and confuse others.

- Do not drink with food in your mouth. If the food is extremely hot, take a discreet quick sip of water to cool off.
- Never leave a spoon in a glass, cup or bowl after stirring.
- Take vitamins and medicine discreetly, preferably away from the table.
- Should you choose not to drink wine, lightly touch your fingertips to the glass rim and softly say, "No, thank you." Do not make a big deal about not drinking. You may raise an empty glass for a toast, but never turn your glass upside down to decline wine.

Serving Food

If you are serving a plate of food to someone, serve from the person's left side. You can bring in two plates at one time. Beverages are served from the right. As you are serving, be sure that you do not touch the eating surface of the plate. Handle silverware and cups by their handles, plates by the rim, and glasses by the base.

- To refill glasses from a pitcher, pour from the right side of the guest. Have a napkin handy to catch any drips. To fill and refill coffee or tea, pick cup and saucer up from the right with your left hand and then pour the beverage with your right hand. Be careful not to touch the pitcher to the guest's beverage glass.
Do not clear the table until everyone is finished. Remove dishes from the left with your left hand. NEVER stack dirty plates. Beverages glasses are removed from the right. Before serving dessert, remove everything except centerpiece, beverages, and the flatware needed for dessert. Water glasses may remain on the table.

Table Tips

- Never put your arms or elbows on the table during the meal. During the meal you may rest your wrist on the table.
- It's a good practice to keep your free hand in your lap.
- Sit up straight and don't slouch at the table.
- If some food falls on the floor discretely pick it up and place it on the edge of your plate. You don't have to touch it again.
- If you must leave the table to use the restroom, quietly say, "Excuse me."
- Feel free to remove alien objects from your mouth with your fingers and place them at the edge of your plate. Do not call attention to this.
- Avoid leaning back in your chair. All four legs of the chair should remain on the floor.
- So you do not reach across the table or across another person, ask the person closest to you to pass the needed item.
- Always pass the salt and pepper together.
- Keep personal items such as your purse, eyeglasses, etc. on your lap or nearby you on the floor, not on the table.
- Do not do any personal grooming at the table, such as picking your teeth. If something gets caught in your teeth, excuse yourself and take care of it in the restroom, not at the table. Use a toothpick in the restroom.
- Most importantly, turn your cell phone off during meal. Even putting it in "vibrate" mode will be a distraction if you get text or phone messages. Your host and hostess and other guests deserve your best attention. The exception to this rule is if you are a medical professional on call.

Passing Food

If you are passing bowls or platters of food at the table, the rules are slightly different.

- Pass serving pieces to the right (counter clockwise). Receive from the person next to you with your left hand and when you pass it, use your right hand. If passing a piece with a spout, offer the handle to the person next to you.
- Food is served from the left and removed from the right and serving platters are offered from the left.
- Liquids are poured and cleared from the right.
- Do not reach in front of a person. Ask the person next to you to pass something to you.
- Say "Please" and "Thank you" frequently.

Starting to Eat

If you are a guest at a dinner party, wait to begin eating both the first course and the dessert until your hostess picks up her fork and begins. At a buffet however, it is okay to begin when the three or four people around you have been served and seated. Try to follow the lead of the host in pacing your eating. Don't eat so fast that you sit with an empty plate. On the other hand, don't eat so slowly that everyone has to wait for you.

- Don't overload your plate. There should be a margin all around your plate.
- Do not cut up your whole meal before eating. Cut one bite at a time. (This does not apply to small children who can't cut for themselves.)
- Do try a little of everything served to you unless you are allergic to it.
- Wait to season food until you taste it.

Eating

- Do eat quietly with your mouth closed and without making smacking, crunching or slurping noises
- Avoid talking when you have food in your mouth. Taking small bites will facilitate conversation.
- Don't blow on hot food.
- Keep your elbows close to your sides when cutting your food.

Silverware

- Generally use a spoon for items served in a bowl and a fork for items served on a plate.
- Eat pie or cake with a fork; eat ice cream or pudding with a spoon.
- It's permissible to eat cookies and brownies with your fingers.
- Never gesture or point with your silverware.
- Always keep your used silverware on your plate. Once it is used, it should never touch the table again.
- At the end of the meal place your used silverware in parallel lines across your plate approximately at the 10:20 clock position. This makes it much easier for the person clearing the table.

Dinner Conversation

This is where heavenly hospitality should shine. This is where you get to know the other people at the table rather than talk about yoursef. As I said earlier, scripture teaches us that we are to consider others as more important than ourself. So let your conversations reflect that and be like salt seasoning. (Colossians 4:6)

- The main point is to let people know you care about them. Begin by asking questions and listening to them share about their family, their job, and their activities.
- Be an engaged listener. The purpose is to get to know your guests better. It's all about them. Listen carefully to what is being said, not what you plan to say next. Try not to "one-up" what the last person said.
- Use encouraging words whenever possible. Be generous with sincere compliments. Anyone can spot a phony.

Leaving the Table

- Guests are free to move to another area when the host or hostess suggests getting up.
- Be sure to express your thanks to the hostess for the meal.
- When you leave the table, asked to be excused or say, "Excuse me for a moment." There is no need to explain why you are leaving.
- At the end of the meal place your silverware across your plate with the knife and fork parallel to each other across the top of the plate.
- It is not good manners to scrape or pile soiled dishes at the table.
- Offer to help clean up after a meal but never insist.

Chapter 5

Overnight Guests

There are many times you will have guests staying overnight in your home. You may also be asked to keep guests overnight as a ministry to others in the faith. The basics remain the same. You don't have to recreate your favorite Bed and Breakfast; just think of the small touches that made you feel comfortable and welcome when away from your home. Provide as many of these small touches as your time, space and budget will allow.

While house guests take more time and energy than dinner guests, the benefits are far reaching. The key is to be prepared ahead of time and set a friendly tone when they first arrive. Attitude is everything. If you make them feel like family, there will be less work for you during their stay. You'll also feel less pressure to impress them.

Your family will greatly benefit from overnight guests. They will learn a great deal about

people, life and other cultures. They will also learn to be comfortable with almost anyone socially. Often missionaries and international guests provide resources for some of their school projects! (My children did many reports on Japan after hosting Japanese house guests.)

Perhaps you have learned from your experiences being a houseguest. Some homes are relaxing to be in but others are downright uncomfortable. The question to ask is, "What would it be like to be a houseguest in my home?" It's not a matter of having a room done by an interior decorator. It's more a matter of it being clean and comfortable.

When your guests first arrive, greet them warmly and offer them a beverage or snack. Offer to help them carry their bags to their room. Show them where everything is: light switches, alarm clock, towels, hair dryer, extra toilet paper, and a helpful basket of forgotten

No Room in the Inn?

What if it's not convenient to have a house guest when someone asks? You may be busy or not feeling up to it. Tell them honestly and graciously, and don't feel guilty. You may simply say, "Now is not a good time for us to have company."

You do not need an "official" guestroom for overnight guest. With a little creativity, you can gather what's needed to make your guest comfortable. Consider investing in an inflatable mattress. Have the bed made up ahead of time so it's ready and fresh. Have pillows and extra blankets handy. It is important to let your guests know ahead of time where they will be sleeping. If they are not comfortable with that, they will need to make other arrangements.

Children

Your children's overnight friends are special, too. Make them feel that way. Although they do not require as much attention to detail, they are going to go home with a distinct impression of a Christian home. Lay down the "ground rules" when they first arrive so that you do not end up having to discipline them. Try to make your home "kid-friendly" by putting away breakables. Ask yourself, "What can I do to make their visit memorable?" Try to send them home thinking their visit was special. Suggest that the children bring sleeping bags to make it easier on you. Because children are sometimes afraid of the dark, it is a good idea to provide a night-light for safety and security.

If you live in a popular tourist area, consider using your home as a way to minister, especially to families with several children for whom vacations may be costly. Prepare a list of sites they may wish to visit. Suggest a schedule and discuss transportation needs. You might wish to pick up a port-a-crib to have on hand for families with babies.

Forgotten Necessities

see pg 90 for a list of what to make available

necessities. If there are any particular tricks to your shower faucets or alarms systems or windows, make sure they know about them, too. Don't forget to show them around the kitchen if they are staying for a few days. They may want to get a drink or have a bowl of cereal.

Ask yourself the question, "What would I want if I slept in this room and spent a day or two here?" It's always welcoming to have a few flowers in a tiny vase on the dresser. That seems to say, "I've been anticipating your arrival!" Flowers don't have to be fancy. A few pansies or daffodils from your yard or African violets from the grocery store will be lovely. A guest refreshment basket is always a welcome surprise and helpful if they should get hungry between meals. Put a couple bottles of water, granola bars and some fresh fruit in the basket.

Before Guests Arrive

Tell them your plans and those of your household.
Tell them what their sleeping arrangements will be.
Tell them what their meal arrangements will be.

The <u>day before</u> they arrive, phone or email to confirm directions, arrival time, departure time, and let them know about weather conditions.

When House Guests Arrive

· Greet guests with a warm welcome.
· Offer a beverage or snack.
· Offer to help them carry their bags to their room.
· Show them where everything is: light switches, alarm clock, towels, hair dryer, extra toilet paper, and guest supply baskets.
· Demonstrate any particular tricks to your shower faucets or alarm systems or windows.
· Show guests where they can store a few personal items. Suggest also where you'd like them to put their suitcase. (Hotel-style luggage racks come in very handy)
· Show them their towels and where they can get an extra towel if needed.
· Show them where to hang their clothes.
· Invite them into the kitchen if they are staying awhile. Show them where the mugs, glasses and cereal bowls are located.
· Point out the coffee maker, coffee, filters, snack or breakfast items
· Discuss schedules and breakfast needs as well as your family routines.
· Offer a house key if appropriate.

Directions Tip

For estimated travel time and directions to your home, check out Map Quest or Google your address on the internet. Then email this link to your guest or print directions and mail them to your guests before they arrive.

Night Lights

Pick several up at the dollar store so your guests do not become confused in an unfamiliar house.

A fancy nightlight makes a nice hostess gift.

Meals for House Guests

Follow the bed and breakfast model and plan for only the first meal of the day. Otherwise, you will feel like you are running a hotel. Just put out a light breakfast of muffins or pastries along with some fruit and coffee. Some items can even be set out the night before. Tell them that they can help themselves when they are ready. If you have an automatic coffee maker set the timer so the coffee is ready when the guests rise.

If you are going to provide dinner, use your crock pot so that dinner will be ready when the guests arrive back at the house in the evening. Keep take-out menus handy so you can order Chinese food or pizza if that works well with your schedules.

Things to do and see

Start collecting tourist brochures for your town and surrounding area. Parks and museums can be an enjoyable way for your guests to spend free time while you are busy. Keep brochures in a folder in your guest room and offer any other suggestions for entertainment. (Include a local map.)

Telephone, Internet and Television

If there is a telephone in the room where your guests will be sleeping, be sure the ringer is turned off so they will not be bothered by calls to your house. Many people travel with their laptop computers and appreciate having access to the internet for business or personal use. If you have wireless internet in your home, leave the security code on a card in the guest room. Many people have televisions for the guests to use to watch news, weather, and sports. Along with the remote control, leave the channel listings on a card.

Pets

Your pets may be cute to you but some people do not like them or are afraid of them. Your guest may have allergies to pet hair or dander. It is always best to keep pets confined when guests arrive.

How to Fix a Sagging Bed

Slip a piece of ½ inch plywood under the mattress.

Guest Room Basics

- Comfortable bed
- Light to read in bed
- Night light
- Mirror
- Alarm clock
- Hangers and place to hang clothes
- Place for personal items
- "Forgotten necessities" basket
- Refreshments basket

Refreshment Basket

A guest refreshment basket is a welcome surprise. Line a basket with a napkin and fill the basket with some bottles of water, snack bars, packages of nuts, and some fresh fruit.

The bedside stand is a nice place to put amenities for your guests. Make sure there's a box of tissues, a scented candle and matches, a devotional guide (like Daily Bread), a Christian magazine, and a Bible. Print out a Bible verse (such as Psalm 3:5 or Psalm 4:8) and lay it on the pillow at night, along with a mint or a piece of chocolate.

Psalm 3:5 (NIV)

I lie down and sleep; I wake again, because the Lord sustains me.

Psalm 4:8 (NIV)

I will lie down and sleep in peace, for you alone, O Lord, make me dwell in safety.

Guest Bathroom

The bathroom your guests use needs to be clean and ready with plenty of fresh towels. If guests are sharing a bathroom with someone else, make sure they know which towels they can use. Perhaps you can tie a pretty ribbon around their towels. They will also need to know where to find more towels if needed. If you are hosting a large group of people, place a towel and wash cloth on the foot of each bed. Be sure to point out where to hang the towels when they are wet. Otherwise, you may find wet towels in a heap on the floor or draped over your furniture which will take the finish off wood furniture. Having an extra hairdryer available for your guests to use is a great idea. Remove unnecessary knick-knacks and personal items from the bathroom counter to give your guests as much space as possible.

Bathroom Basics

- · Towels
- · Bath mat
- · Forgotten Necessities Basket
- · Extra toilet paper

Forgotten Necessities Basket

- · Hotel samples (lotions, shampoos, conditioners etc.)
- · new toothbrush
- · small tube of toothpaste
- · deodorant sample
- · shower cap
- · feminine protection products
- · mending kit
- · disposable razor
- · disposable drinking cups

Linens

Guest room linens should always be fresh and clean. Washing them in hot water kills mites and germs. Use a fabric softener or dryer sheet when drying your sheets to make them smell nice.

Saying Goodbye

When your guests leave at the end of their visit, remind them to check the closet and bathroom for anything they may have left behind. Help them with their luggage. Walk your guests to the front door and tell them how much you enjoyed their visit. Offer a prayer for a refreshed spirit and a safe journey home. Wave as they drive away.

Being a Pleasant Overnight Guest
Here are some tips for when you are a house guest.

Before You Arrive
Communicate clearly when you expect to arrive and when you will leave. Inform your host of any other plans you may have while you will be in their home. If you plan to take them out for a meal while you are there, let them know ahead of time so they will not have something planned. (They will almost always welcome this kind gesture.) Let your host know of any allergies, or special food needs you may have. Ask them what the local weather will be, so you can pack accordingly.

Illnesses
If you or someone traveling with you becomes ill along the way, don't take the germs to the host family. Make other arrangements. If you become ill during your stay, do everything possible not to spread the germs and to take care of yourself without being a burden.

Pets
Do not bring your pets. Your host may have allergies or may not appreciate Fido or Miss Kitty. Take your pet to a "pet hotel" or hire a professional pet sitter or a responsible neighborhood boy or girl to watch your animal.

Arrival
Try to give your host an accurate arrival time and if it changes, communicate the change to them. This is especially important if they are picking you up at a train or bus station or an airport. Cell phones make it easy to connect if you discover that you will be late. Be sure to exchange telephone numbers ahead of time. Arrive at a reasonable time of day. Inquire about and take into consideration rush hour traffic. If you are flying in and the airport is more than a half-hour from your host's home, offer to rent a car or use a taxi.

> The best houseguest is an undemanding houseguest!

During Your Stay

- If your hosts remove their shoes in their house, do likewise.
- Be sensitive to your hosts' schedule and plans. Do not expect your hosts to entertain you all the time.
- Be as unobtrusive as possible.
- Give your host some "down time". Plan some time on your own.
- Do not keep your hosts up late at night talking. Excuse yourself for bed at a reasonable hour.
- Try to give a little attention to each family member in your host's household.
- If a child or family member is displaced for you to use the bedroom, remember to thank them with a special token of appreciation.
- Offer to help with household chores. Follow your host's example and look for opportunities to help. Do not just ask what you can do; pitch in and help with things like clearing the table. Put your snack dishes in the dishwasher.
- Do not use appliances and electronics without asking and getting directions for use.
- If you break or lose something, fix or replace it.
- Ask to use their phone. Be sure to pay for any long distance calls you make. If you do not have a cell phone, do not monopolize their house line.
- Do not leave your personal belongings all over their house.

Hostess Gift Suggestion

If you are staying several days, you may want to wait until you see what your host's or hostess's tastes are. Then, shop for your gift.

Mealtime

If you are arriving around a meal time, indicate your intentions. Consider getting a bite to eat along the way so you will not trouble them for a special meal. Let them know if you'll be late. Encourage them to eat without you. Provide at least one meal out for your hosts.

Your Room

Keep your room neat and tidy. Make your bed each morning. Do not spread your belongings all over the house or bathroom. Never leave wet towels around, especially draped over furniture. Hang them up in the bathroom. Try to keep most of your things in your suitcase. Do not eat or drink in your room if it is not the custom of the host or hostess.

Leaving

The morning you plan to leave, ask the hostess if she would like you to strip the bed and bring all the linens to the laundry area. Wipe up the bathroom if there are cleaning products available. Be sure everything is returned to its original location. Look around for your belongings.

Hostess gifts

Generally your gift as a house guest should be more substantial than the gift you might give for only a meal. If you forget to bring a gift, find a local gift shop and pick something up. Stop by a bakery or a roadside stand. Pick up a floral plant or some fresh produce. Breakfast baked goods are almost always a welcome gift and a help to the hostess. Offer your gift shortly after your arrival, especially if it is perishable.

If you keep thank you notes tucked in your suitcase, you can write them before you leave. Leave your note and gift on the bed before you leave as a surprise for the hostess.

House Guest Gift Ideas

- Flowers (sent ahead of time) from a florist
- Set of guest towels or a pretty hand towel
- Placemats and napkins set
- A basket of lotions and bubble bath
- Lap throw or afghan
- Small plant (like mum for fall or azalea for spring)
- Board games, beach towels, or guest book if you are staying at their vacation home or beach house
- Breakfast or tea basket, filled with "goodies".
- A gift basket (see below ideas)

Gift Baskets

Gift baskets, make great gifts to say "thank you". Line your basket with a napkin, tea towel, colored tissue paper, or a doily. Types of baskets to give can include:

- Coffee or Tea basket: favorite coffee and tea plus two mugs or a pretty tea cup and saucer, cheese spread, jam, crackers, cookie or scone mix, or chocolates
- Kitchen basket (also great for new neighbors): kitchen towel, wooden spoon/ spatula, favorite recipe with a sample, an encouraging Scripture verse or one of your favorite music CDs
- Bottles of lotion, creams or bubble bath
- Stationery basket: postcards, stationery, and thank you notes, plus stamps
- Man of the House Basket: a car care basket (sponge, soap, glass cleaner, whisk broom) or a shoe care basket (brush, leather cleaner, brown and black shoe polish, polishing cloth)

Gift Tip

When shopping, keep an eye out for gift items on sale. Start a gift drawer or shelf so you always have something on hand

Christians have more reason to celebrate and show love than anybody else. This next section of the book will give you lots of creative ideas for showing heavenly hospitality during holidays and at other special times of year. Don't forget to check out the web site too; as new ideas will be posted there from time to time.

Holiday Open House

The name alone tells you what this is all about. Your guests are invited to come any time between the hours printed on the invitation. The Christmas season is a particularly good time to host an Open House because people receive so many invitations!

Open houses often use a "Regrets Only" form of reply rather than the typical "R.S.V.P."

Here are some Open House themes to try:

- Christmas Carol Sing
- New Year's Day - bring an appetizer and a resolution to share
- Graduations, retirements or special anniversaries
- Meet the new neighbors
- Meet the newlyweds (when the wedding is in a different city)

There are plenty of things to celebrate in the fall. Start off by having a Labor Day Picnic and find out what your neighbors did over the summer.

Back to School Celebrations

The first day of school is exciting for moms as well as for the children. Throw a party! Have all the neighborhood moms over for coffee after they put their children on the bus or finish carpools. Throw an End of Summer - Back to School party for the children in your neighborhood and decorate with a school supply theme. Gather some friends who may not know the Lord for a Coffee, make up "back-to-school" packs for the poor. Take them together down to the city mission or Salvation Army. It may be the first time some of them ever visited that part of the city or the first time they've done this sort of thing. This is an excellent example of a pre-evangelistic event.

First Day of Fall Celebrations

Give a First day of Fall (September 21st) Coffee or Dessert. Decorate with a potted mum and colorful leaves gathered from your yard. In October, invite some ladies to go for a walk in the park followed by refreshments at your house or a nearby coffee shop. Ask them to share their Fall memories from growing up. You will get to know them better and they will feel loved and cared about. This may lead to a "walking group" where the relationships will continue to grow. You may even want to have a speaker talk about the "Fall" of our lives or the value of exercise.

Halloween

See the children's section for ideas. Hand out your candy with attractive tracts or the pumpkin poem which is found in the children's chapter.

Thanksgiving Gathering

Thanksgiving is another holiday that can be used as a relationship building event or as a sharing event. It is especially interesting to Internationals (people from other countries now living in the United States). Most foreign countries do not have a holiday like this and are always interested in historical and cultural events that are unique to our country. Thanksgiving goes back to the very founding of our nation. Even many secular Americans today have no idea that we are supposed to be thankful to God. Again, here is a holiday where we Christians need not be afraid to share our faith.

At one event, I had a friend dress up in a rented costume as Deacon Cushman, one of the leaders in Plymouth Colony. He knocked at my door and came in-- right out of the 1700's, and quoted the sermon located on this book's companion web site. The guests were excited and surprised to hear about the Pilgrims' strong faith.

There are many ways that you can approach a Thanksgiving gathering. You can invite people to join your family's traditional dinner or have a Dessert party and serve light refreshments like pies, or pumpkin and cranberry bread. If your event is a Coffee, Tea or Dessert, invite your guests to fill their cups and come sit down to hear your speaker. This talk can also be used after a Thanksgiving meal in your home.

As a reminder of how hard it was for the Pilgrims to make it through that first winter, put five kernels of dried corn on everyone's plate. As they sit down to dinner, you can tell them that this was the Pilgrims' daily ration each day through that first winter. It is a powerful illustration of what a miracle God performed (see pg 105).

Often at family Thanksgiving dinners we put a Thanksgiving related Bible verse at everyone's place at the table or on the back of their place card. Before serving dessert, we have each person read their verse and say one thing that they are thankful for this year. The following are some suggested verses which are also photo-copy ready for you on pg 98.

I Thessalonians 5:16-18
I Chronicles 16:8-9, 12
Psalm 77:11-14
Psalm 92:1-5
Psalm 95:1-5
Psalm 75:1
Psalm 106:1
Philippians 4:6-7
Colossians 3:16-17

Thanks for the Memories Basket

Take a pretty basket and fill it with duplicate copies of family photos from the past year. Put the basket on the Thanksgiving table. After dinner, guests are invited to browse through the basket and take whatever pictures they'd like. It's a great way to remember what to be thankful for. Make it a family tradition that everyone will look forward to. They will love being able to take home their thankful memories.

For a good Thanksgiving Day Punch see pg 227 of the recipe section

1 Chronicles 16:8-9, 12

Give thanks to the Lord, call on his name; make known among the nations what he has done. Sing to him, sing praise to him; tell of all his wonderful acts. Remember the wonders he has done, his miracles, the judgements he pronounced. (NIV)

1 Thessalonians 5:16-18

Be joyful always; pray continually; give thanks in all circumstances, for this is God's will for you in Christ Jesus. (NIV)

Philippians 4:6

Do not be anxious about anything, but in everything, by prayer and petition, with thanksgiving, present your requests to God. (NIV)

Psalm 77:11-14

I will remember the deeds of the Lord; yes, I will remember your miracles of long ago. I will meditate on all your works and consider all your mighty deeds. Your ways, O God, are holy. What god is so great as our God? You are the God who performs miracles; you display your power among the peoples. (NIV)

Colossians 3:16-17

Let the word of Christ dwell in you richly as you teach and admonish one another with all wisdom, and as you sing psalms, hymns and spiritual songs with gratitude in your hearts to God. And whatever you do, whether in word of deed, do it all in the name of the Lord Jesus, giving thanks to God the Father through him. (NIV)

Psalm 92:1-5

It is good to praise the Lord and make music to your name, O Most High, to proclaim your love in the morning and your faithfullness at night, to the music of the ten-stringed lyre and the melody of the harp. For you make me glad by your deeds, O Lord, I sing for joy at the work of your hands. How great are your works, O Lord, how profound your thoughts! (NIV)

Psalm 95:1-5

Come, let us sing for joy to the Lord; let us shout aloud to the Rock of our salvation. Let us come before him with thanksgiving and extol him with music and song. For the Lord is a great God, the great King above all gods. In his hand are the depths of the earth, and the mountain peaks belong to him. The sea is his, for he made it, and his hands formed the dry land. (NIV)

Psalm 75:1

We give thanks to you, O God, we give thanks, for your Name is near; men tell of your wonderful deeds. (NIV)

Psalm 106:1

Praise the Lord. Give thanks to the Lord, for he is good, his love endures forever. (NIV)

Thanksgiving Ideas

- Give the whole family a chance to understand thankfulness by making a food basket for the poor, volunteering to serve a meal at the local mission or adopting a needy family for the holidays.
- As guests arrive for dinner, have them write on a slip of paper what they're thankful for and place it in a bowl. Later, at the table, make a game of getting everyone to try to guess who wrote each slip of paper.
- Make the children's table more fun by using a paper table cloth and giving each of them crayons or markers. Trace each child's hand and let them turn it into a turkey. Have leaves they could trace and color. Print out copies of coloring book pages or games.
- Place Card Ideas: Instead of writing names, put old photos of each family member at their place. Everyone will want to take theirs home after they've shared something special about when the photo was taken.
- Put on a crock pot of hot spiced cider ahead of time so the house smells good and you have a warm drink to hand to people as they arrive.

Items that you can duplicate and send home with your guests

- Blessings Mix recipe
- Turkey "cookie" gift favors
- The story of the 5 kernels of corn
- List if table verses to attach to place cards
- Deacon Cushman Sermon on the first Thanksgiving (from web site)

Celebrate with us as we give thanks for this year's blessings!

Time:

Date:

Bring:

Dress:

Location:

Please RSVP to:

copy this thanksgiving invite two to a page on a color copier or download it from the website to print out.

Blessings Mix

This is a great "goodie bag" to hand out at a fall party, Halloween or Thanksgiving. It's a yummy treat with a wonderful message. Print the information below on a piece of paper and attach it to the bag of treats. (Punch a hole in the corner of the card.)

Blessings Mix:

Bugles®: Cornucopia, a symbol of our nation's abundance

Pretzels: Arms folded in prayer; a freedom sought by those who founded our country

Indian Candy Corn: This represents the sacrifices of the pilgrim's first winter: food was so scarce that settlers survived on just 5 kernels of corn a day

Nuts & Seeds: Promise of a future harvest; one we will reap only if seeds are planted and tended with diligence

Dried Fruits: Harvest gifts from our bountiful land

M & M's®: Memories of those who came before us to lead us into a blessed future

Hershey's Kisses®: The love of family and friends that sweetens our life

Thanksgiving Favor

This is a cute idea to put at each person's place on your dinner table. Children love these. Here is what you need to buy:
Chocolate Filled Oreos
Candy corn
Crispy Rice Balls (made with Rice Krispies® treats recipe from cereal box)
- 40 large marshmallows
- 3 tablespoons of melted butter
- 6 cups of Rice Krispies®
- Can of chocolate icing to glue turkeys together

The Five Kernels of Corn

The Five Kernels of Corn Story:

This tradition has roots deep into American history, back to the second Thanksgiving dinner in Plymouth in the year 1622.

We all have heard stories of that first Thanksgiving dinner. These stories tell of how the Mayflower, after being blown off course by a severe North Atlantic storm, landed at Cape Cod, far north of the intended destination in Virginia. The Pilgrims were unable to sail south because of unfavorable winds and concluded it was God's plan for them to stay where they landed. God provided for them and sustained them in the wilderness.

They were surprised to discover cleared fields and to meet an Indian named Squanto who spoke English. Their first harvest was so plentiful that Governor Bradford declared a day of public thanksgiving to thank God for his miraculous provision and protection - the First Thanksgiving! It lasted for three days. Governor Bradford's diary said of Squanto, "He became a special instrument of God sent for our good...He showed us how to plant corn, where to catch fish and procure other commodities,"

The next winter was very hard. More settlers had come and they ran so low on food provisions that they had to limit the food rations to only 5 kernels of corn per person for each day!

So on the second Thanksgiving their first course was only 5 kernels of corn on an empty plate in order to remind them of how miraculously the Lord had brought them through that difficult winter.

It's hard for us to imagine getting along on such a small amount of food. Indeed today we have very much to be thankful for. Let's go around the table and share one thing that each of us is thankful for.

This story was adapted from The Light and the Glory by Peter Marshall. The book can be bought at petermarshallministries.com

Deer Wood
Acres

PSALM 42:1
"AS THE DEER PANTETH FOR WATER,
SO MY SOUL LONGETH AFTER THEE;
THOU ALONE ART MY HEART'S
DESIRE AND I LONG TO WORSHIP THEE."

Chapter 7

Winter Events

Here are some enjoyable occasions to celebrate with your friends and neighbors. You will be surprised how glad people are to join in your fun.

· First Snow
· First Day of Winter/Winter Solstice on December 21st
· Snowed-in or Ice Storm Parties
· Bowl Games or Super Bowl Parties
· Christmas Outreach Events
· Christmas Family Gatherings
· New Year's Eve Game Night
· New Year's Day Brunch or Open House
· Valentine's Day
· St. Patrick's Day

First Snow Day Parties

After your neighbors have shoveled their sidewalks and driveways, invite them over for hot chocolate and pancakes.

Snowed-in Party with the Neighbors

A friend always had the ingredients to make chili and cornbread in her pantry. Every time she was snowed-in or had an ice storm, she would invite all her neighbors come over for supper. They all looked forward to it. Several families ended up accepting Christ and started going to church with them. It all started with snow and chili!

Football Parties

Use the big games that are on TV as a reason to gather friends. Have simple parties to cheer on your team or just a good excuse to relax and have fun together. Ask your guests to dress in the colors of their favorite team. Put on a pot of chili or order some pizza. Just being together is a great way to build relationships for a future event where the Gospel may be presented.

Christmas

There are many ideas for using Christmas to present the Gospel. Invite singles and Internationals who are alone on Christmas to join you and your family. Have an impromptu tree decorating or Christmas caroling party. One year I phoned a Jewish friend and she jumped at the idea of helping me decorate my tree. I was able to answer a lot of her questions about Christ as we hung the ornaments. She was thrilled to see Christmas up close.

Ideas to Use with Christmas Guests

Christmas is the one time of year when we do not have to make any excuses for sharing Christ. No matter how secular our world tries to make this holiday, it is still the day Christians celebrate Jesus' birthday. There is no end to the ideas we can use for this holiday. Evangelistic Coffees and Desserts are simple occasions to share the Gospel. Things can be simple and even done on the spur-of-the-moment. Drop by a neighbor's house with a plate of goodies and invite them to your church's service or program.

One Christmas Eve I took a plate of Christmas cookies to our neighbors, Philip and Sean. Philip answered the door and gratefully received the homemade goodies. They were new to the neighborhood so we had had little contact with them. They didn't seem like the type of young people who would be interested in Christian things. I was surprised at myself when I blurted out a last minute invitation to join us for our church Christmas

Eve service. Then, I was shocked at his response. Philip got all excited and said that as a child he used to go to church on Christmas Eve. He said he would love to join us but first he would have to check with his partner, Sean, before committing for both of them.

Both young men rode to church that night with us and returned to our home for Christmas cookies and hot fudge sundaes in front of our fireplace. It not only became a tradition for the remainder of their tenure in our neighborhood but it led to many deep spiritual conversations and many opportunities to share the love of Christ. These two men probably would have never come to our church without an invitation. We later even shared Easter services and brunch.

Never second guess where the Holy Spirit may be at work. He's full of surprises. Even though Philip and Sean moved away, we still stay in touch by email. The day before they moved, I stopped by to say good bye. I stood on that same front porch and hugged Philip saying that I had a special, supernatural love for them and would sorely miss them. He hugged me back and said he knew what I meant. He thanked me for being such a good neighbor. He added that because of our times together, he had decided that looking for a church would be one of the first things he would do after moving and thanked me for reconnecting him with spiritual things. The next morning my husband drove him to the airport and gave him a copy of The Purpose Driven Life to read on the plane. He was very glad to receive it and promised to read it.

Christmas Ideas

Good News Cookies

Print the following on a pretty card and attach the card to a plate of Christmas cookies. Use cookies cutters in such shapes as angels, stars, trees, hearts and bells.

An **angel** brought the glorious news to the shepherds that a Savior had been born. Wise men followed a bright **star** to the manger where Jesus lay. They brought precious gifts much like the gifts we have under our **tree**. The best Christmas gift of all time was Jesus! God sent His only Son that whoever accepts Him into their **heart** will have life everlasting and go to heaven. Let the **bells** ring out this holiday season as we celebrate Jesus" birthday and God's greatest gift to us.

Adult Christmas Dinner Party Idea

At a dinner party ask the following question to stimulate table conversation:

"Which Christmas or Christmas present do you remember most?"

Children's Christmas Party

Better than decorating cookies by yourself, have a Christmas party for the children in your neighborhood. It can be as simple as reading a children's Christmas book and serving cookies. Go to the Children's Parties section of this book for ideas.

Cookie Exchange Party

For years the cookie exchange party has been a favorite with women because it makes their baking easier. Each guest bakes a double or triple batch of her favorite cookies and brings them along with the recipe and an empty cookie tin. The platters of cookies are laid out on a big table. After everyone arrives, each guest walks around the table and puts in her tin the same number of cookies that she brought. Everyone goes home with a wide variety of cookies to enjoy with her holiday guests, family or neighbors. After the cookies have been exchanged and a few are enjoyed over a cup of coffee, a Gospel message can be shared.

Ornament Exchange Party

Many of us are used to the normal ornament exchange gifts, at parties but my friend Karen came up with something clever. After attending one of my "Heavenly Hospitality Workshops", she had an O.U.T. ornament exchange. Everyone brought an Obnoxious, Ugly or Tacky ornament wrapped in beautiful paper and played the exchange game where everyone takes a number and they pick their gift or steal a gift in order. It produced more laughter than she had heard in her house in years. At the end when each woman was looking at her ugly ornament and trying to figure out just what on earth she was going to do with it, Karen shared the following:

"Please don't throw this ugly ornament away. Find a spot on the back of your tree where you can hang it. Use it as a reminder that we are not perfect. We actually need Christmas and the Christ of Christmas."

Then she went on to share the meaning of the Christmas story and what Jesus is to her family. It turned out to be a very creative way to introduce people to what Christmas is really all about.

Gifts from Jesus

Put gift boxes or ornament boxes at each place at your dinner party or Christmas table representing gifts we get from Jesus at Christmas. Print out the verses listed here on a piece of paper. Cut the verses apart and put one slip of paper in each box to represent one of the gifts we receive from Jesus when we invite him into our lives. At some time during the meal, have each guest read aloud what their gift from Jesus is.

Before each gift is read, the host can read the introduction printed below.

"The moment we invite Jesus into our lives, He gives us more gifts than we can comprehend. The Bible contains over 3,000 promises from Him and the Word of God itself is a gift. He didn't just come into our lives and then expect us to figure out the rest on our own but He gave us a "how to" manual for our lives. That's the Bible!

These little boxes at each of your places at the table contain a gift to you from Jesus. Open them and share one of the gifts we've all received from Jesus with us around the table."

(Make copies of the next page and cut it into strips for your gift boxes.)

I had only intended to use this idea with our family one Christmas. However, I had left these gift boxes mixed in with my table decorations. Later that week we had another family over for dinner. One of the children noticed the box in front of her plate and opened it. Soon everyone was checking to see what was in their box. What was a forgotten idea, intended only for my family, soon became the topic for our table discussion. An unplanned opportunity to share the Gospel occurred spontaneously because of a curious child.

Peace – No matter what's happening in life around us, Jesus gives us a peace that others don't experience. "Peace I leave with you; my peace I give you. I do not give to you as the world gives. Do not let your hearts be troubled and do not be afraid." John 14:27 NIV.

Joy – No matter how sad a situation may be Jesus gives us an unexplainable inner joy. "I have told you this so that my joy may be in you and that your joy may be complete." John 15:11 NIV.

Hope – The world's situation may be harrowing and appear to be hopeless but Jesus gives us a hope in the future because he is always in control. In Jeremiah 29:11 NIV he promises us a future of hope. "For I know the plans I have for you," declares the Lord, "plans to prosper you and not to harm you, plans to give you hope and a future."

Companionship – Jesus promises, unlike people in our lives, that he will never leave us. "God has said, Never will I leave you; never will I forsake you." Hebrews 13:5 NIV. He also sent us the Holy Spirit for all time. Jesus said, "I will ask the Father, and he will give you another Counselor to be with you forever - the Spirit of Truth." John 14:16-17 NIV.

Heaven – When Jesus left earth, he said in John 14 that he was going to prepare a place for us in heaven where there are many mansions and the streets were paved with gold.

Eternal Life – Eternal life begins the moment we ask him into our lives. "God has given us eternal life, and this life is in his Son. He who has the Son has life; he who does not have the Son of God does not have life. I write these things to you who believe in the name of the Son of God so that you may KNOW that you have eternal life." I John 5:11-13 NIV.

Forgiveness – Jesus gives us freedom from ourselves and things that displease Him. "The Lord our God is merciful and forgiving, even though we have rebelled against him." Daniel 9:9. "All the prophets testify about him that everyone who believes in him receives forgiveness of sins through his name." Acts 10:43 NIV.

A New Family – The moment you asked Christ into your life, you were adopted into the family of God. "To all who received Him, to those who believed in His name, He gave the right to become children of God." John 1:12 NIV.

Hot Line to God – Jeremiah 33:3 says, "Call unto me and I will answer and show you great and unsearchable things you do not know." NIV.

Road Map & How-to Manual for Life – The word of God "is a lamp to my feet and a light to my path." Ps.119:105. God's word is also "profitable for teaching, reproof, correction and training in righteousness." II Tim. 3:16 NIV.

Love – "We know how much God loves us because we have felt his love." I John.4:16 LB.

Christmas Crackers

British "crackers" are a fun addition to a Christmas table. Each guest recieves a small toy, paper hat, or funny saying after pulling open one of these small favors with a loud 'crack!' They are available at World Market, Pier 1, and other stores.

Christmas symbols

At one Christmas coffee, we were eagerly sharing our Christmas traditions. Suddenly my curious Pakistani neighbor jumped in and asked, "What's the significance of the toy train going around the Christmas tree?" We all burst out in laughter because none of us had ever thought about it. As people continue to try to secularize our special holiday, it becomes all the more important that we look for ways to, unapologetically, bring the focus back on Jesus Christ -- the real reason for the season.

Print out the following Origins of Christmas Traditions on decorative holiday paper and use these as hand outs or a take home souvenir of your Christmas event. Use them, if needed, to stimulate your guests to share their own special holiday traditions. This is especially helpful with Internationals because they are curious about our Christmas traditions.

The Origins Of Christmas Traditions

Trees

Martin Luther was reportedly the first person to have a Christmas tree in his home in the 1600's. Germans brought the custom to America. In 1841, during Queen Victoria's reign, she brought Christmas trees from Germany to England to delight her young son. In 1850 a picture of their tree appeared in a British magazine and the custom spread through England.

Evergreens

Pine boughs signify the everlasting life that Jesus, the Messiah, brought.

Lights on Trees

This idea also originated with Martin Luther. On a cold winter night, Luther was returning from speaking in a country church. As he walked through the fresh snow, he saw twinkling stars. These reminded him of stars the shepherds must have seen on the first Christmas Eve. He put candles on his tree to twinkle and brighten his home.

Stars

Stars are to remind us of the Star of David for the promised Messiah, or Star of Bethlehem, which led the 3 kings to baby Jesus.

Candle

Candles remind us that Jesus is the light of the world.

Bells These signify the joy Jesus brought.

Candy Canes These remind us of the shepherd's crook.

Christmas Colors

The color RED is to remind us of the blood of Jesus shed on Calvary as the sacrifice for sin. GREEN reminds us of the everlasting life available to those who put their trust in Jesus.

Wreaths

Wreaths are circles, with no beginning or end, representing the Eternal life that Jesus gives.

Holly

Spiked leaves represent the crown of thorns Jesus wore and red berries represent His blood shed for us.

Candy Cane Handout

The candy cane can be a symbol of Christmas. Use the story below to share the glorious birth of Jesus Christ and to point to His desire to be our Savior and Lord. Print it on some decorative holiday paper with candy cane designs. Attach a small candy cane to it or place it beside a bowl of candy canes for your guests to take home as they leave your party. An excellent idea for children's parties is to read the book called, The Candy Maker's Gift by David & Helen Haidle. It, too, is full of children's party ideas.

The Legend of the Candy Cane

The candy cane is a shepherd's crook. The shepherds saw the star and the heavenly host of angels that night Christ was born. The shepherds visited Mary, Joseph and the baby Jesus and were the first to give him glory and praise.

Shepherds used the crook to lead and guide their sheep. A good shepherd served his sheep. Christ is our shepherd. He calls us to be good shepherds.

The colors of the candy cane remind us of Jesus' life and sacrifice for us. The white is for His purity. The small red stripes for the pain He endured for us. The large red stripe is for His ultimate sacrifice -- His death on the cross that we might all have eternal life with God.

The taste of the candy cane is sharp, clean and refreshing.
The cane can be broken and shared with others.
Jesus offers new life; sharp, clean and refreshing.
He was born to be broken and shared with others.

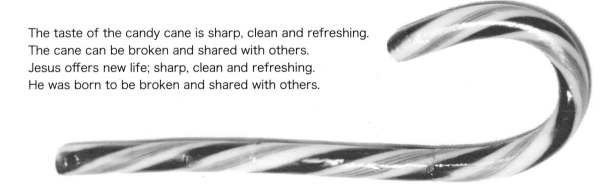

Merry Christmas

Come Celebrate the season with us!

Given By:

Date:
Time:

Location:

Please RSVP to:

Download and print this Christmas gathering invitation from www.EntertainingForEternity.com

Origins of Gift Giving

The Romans predated the Christians in giving small gifts during the winter months. Perhaps it was to cheer friends during the winter doldrums. The origin of Christmas gifts began when the early Christians were inspired by the gifts that the three kings brought to baby Jesus.

The first Christmas gifts were handmade. They were from the heart, costing only time and personal talent. My very favorite gifts over the years and things that I treasure most are the handmade ones.

Handmade Gift Ideas

· Baked Goods

· Original poems, stories and paintings

· Coupons for help with various chores around the house

· Photo calendars or scrapbooks

· Ornaments and decorations

Easy Evangelistic Christmas Coffees or Desserts

You'll never have an easier time of year to invite people to your home to hear a solid presentation of what Jesus is all about. Christmas after all is Christ's birthday! He truly is "the reason for the season". The following pages contain two sample talks that your speaker could use. They are tried and true and really effective. Remember not to be the speaker at your own party but to ask a friend. It will take the pressure and focus off of you and give you a chance to interact with your guests.

I have used the following talk with two different ladies events. One was a large Christmas brunch at a community country club and the other occasion was a ladies Tea at a church. Both times the ladies were thrilled at the end of the talk when they opened their gift and discovered a compact mirror. When they see their reflection the mirror illustrates to them the point of the talk, what God wants for Christmas. The event will end with an air of excitement and anticipation as they open their wrapped gifts.

Your speaker could also use a scented candle or scented potpourri for the gift that you hold out during the beginning of the talk. The parallel with what Jesus does in one's life is amazing. Don't be afraid of a pause or hesitation when the gift is offered. No one wants to look greedy. Simply hold it out and say something like, "This is a real gift. Don't be shy. I'm not going to go on until someone comes up and takes it." Be sure to take notice of the recipient's first name from her nametag so the speaker can refer personally to her as the talk progresses.

After any evangelical gathering, don't be shy about asking for comment cards. It's the only way you will find out where the Lord was at work during your party. Remember everyone likes to give his or her opinion. Be sure to have some Christmas music playing while they fill the cards out. Be clear where you want your guests to leave their cards. A pretty basket with a Christmas bow is always nice.

January is a perfect time to offer a follow-up Bible Discussion Group. Social schedules are usually emptier and the dreary winter weather is a good excuse to gather over hot coffee or tea in front of a fire. Don't call your event a Bible Study as it may scare some people away. Recently when I asked my next door neighbor to come to my Bible Study she was worried because she didn't know anything about the Bible. I told her that was great because that was exactly why I was having the group.

Take some time and read over the following suggested talk. Ask the Lord to show you how you could use one this Christmas. Don't be limited by the season. There is another Sample Talk on the web site that would be appropriate for men as well.

Take Home Booklet
You may also want to have copies of a booklet for them to take home or to give them on a follow up appointment. An excellent choice is Campus Crusade's pamphlet: <u>Would You Like to Know God Personally?</u>

See pg 190 for more information on making and using comment cards.

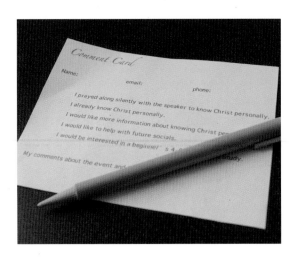

See pg 191 for more information on using this booklet

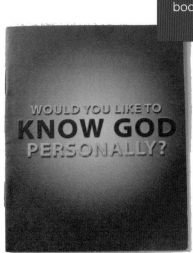

You are Invited
to a
Christmas Gathering

Given By:
Address:

Time:

Date:

Please RSVP to:

A friend will share some inspiring
thoughts on Christmas

Download and print this
Christmas gathering invitation,
cut apart, then poke holes and
put a tiny red ribbon on your
wreath!

Sample Christmas talk
What God wants for Christmas

I have enjoyed hearing the traditions many of you have shared. Recently, I asked my own grown children what they remembered our family traditions to be. When all three mentioned the decorating of Christmas cookies, they were thinking about those wonderful iced cookie cutter cookies. It became a Christmas eve tradition that left my kitchen sticky from one end to the other. (Instead you may personalize this using a couple of sentences on your own tradition here.)

There is one universal tradition that we all celebrate; the presents. Certainly the giving and receiving of gifts is big part of what we remember about Christmas. Let's pause for a moment and think about the dynamics of gift giving!

Giver: the giver of the gift is someone who makes a sacrifice of money, time...
Gift: a gift is free, no obligation, no strings attached, usually serves a purpose or fulfills a need
Receiver: person who chooses to receive the gift, opens the gift, uses the gift as his or her own

Now, I have a gift in my hands.
I am the giver of this gift.

In order to complete my illustration, I need someone to receive my gift, someone to come and take the gift and claim it as his or her own.... (Wait for someone to take the gift)

While _____ opens the gift, let's review the characteristics of gift giving:
I was the giver of the gift. There was some sacrifice involved in picking it out, wrapping it, and a little sacrifice in terms of money.

Then there is the gift. It is free. Did you see _____ give me any money? I don't know if he (or she) even really deserves the gift; but it was given with no conditions or strings attached. Hopefully, it will serve a purpose this Christmas season and will be a special reminder of our Christmas gathering today.

___ gets to keep the gift because he (or she) is the one who claimed it as his (or her) own.

(Use a scented candle or potpouri.)

My reason for going through this illustration of the elements of gift giving is that _____ has asked me to share about the most precious and greatest gift that was ever given. It was this gift that got the whole Christmas thing going in the first place.

"For God so loved the world that He gave His only Son, that whoever believes in Him would not perish, but would have eternal life."   (John 3:16 NIV)

These words are from the book of John in the Bible and may or may not be familiar to you.

Let's take a moment and reflect on what these words from the Bible mean:

God – who is God? The Bible teaches God is the Creator and Sustainer of the universe. He created everything in the world including you and me. And because He created us, He knows everything about us. He knows what fills your heart with joy, and He knows what causes you to grieve. He knows your loneliness. He knows your frustrations and your hurts. He knows what makes you laugh. He knows all of these things because He made you. He created you and me to have fellowship with Him forever.

And how do we respond to God's plan for us? We often turn our backs on God and choose to go our own way rather than God's way. The reason we do this is because we seek fulfillment for our lives, not in God, the Creator of the universe, but in the things He has created. We worship intellect, material things, money, and other people. We worship the things that God made rather than worshiping the Creator.

These things separate us from God, take his place in our lives and are called sin. Anything that separates us from God is called sin. The Bible tells us, "All of us have sinned and fallen short of the glory of God." (Romans 3:23 NIV) None of us are perfect.

"God so loved the world that He gave"(John 3:16 NIV)--Some 2000 years ago God gave His Son Jesus to be born in a stable. When I was a little girl, I thought a stable was the cute little red barn with the sweet smelling animals and the clean hay that I saw in pictures. It wasn't until I was much older that I learned that the stable was actually a dark, damp cave where animals were kept. They were not very sweet smelling, and the hay was probably not very clean. The very place where He slept was actually the animals' feeding trough. Our children are born under conditions fit for a king, and Jesus, the King of Creation, was born under conditions fit for an animal.

Fortunately, Jesus didn't stay in the manger. He grew to be a man and lived on this earth for about 33 years. While He was on earth, He said and did many amazing things which are recorded in the Bible. They are also written in secular, historical books written during that time.

One of the amazing things Jesus did was make a very unique claim. He claimed something that no other religious leader or philosopher has ever claimed. He said, "I am the Way, the Truth, and the Life. No one comes to the Father except through Me." (John 14:6 NIV) He could say that because of something He did – this is something that can be difficult to comprehend and completely understand.

He willingly chose to die. He willingly chose to die on the cross for every sin that you and I would ever commit! You see the Bible says that the result of sin is spiritual death and separation from a holy God. Old Testament Judaism required a blood sacrifice for sin.

Every year on the Day of Atonement the Jewish High Priest would sacrifice a lamb for the sins that the Jews committed that year. Instead of a "lamb", Jesus became Our Lamb. To be the sacrificial lamb in our story, He died on the cross in our place. Jesus paid the penalty. He shed his blood so that you and I would no longer be separated from God because of our sin. Because Jesus willingly laid down His life, we can have forgiveness for our sin and have fellowship with God restored forever. How can we know this is true? Jesus rose from the dead! He's alive! The Bible tells us He sits now at the right hand of God praying for us; for you and for me. No other religious leader or philosopher has ever risen from the dead.

Now let's take a minute and review the gift illustration:

1. Who is the giver of the greatest gift? God. He gave us a gift that involved the greatest amount of love and sacrifice; his very own son.

2. The gift was Jesus Christ. His purpose was to restore our broken relationship with God and assure us of eternal life. The gift of Jesus Christ is free and cannot be earned. Even though most of us try to live good lives, we will never deserve Him. However, no matter how much we have sinned, the gift of Jesus Christ will never be withheld from us. This is where my gift illustration breaks down. I only had one gift to give and only one of you could accept it. But the gift of Jesus Christ is offered to each one of us.

3. Think about the third characteristic. We've looked at the giver of the gift, the gift itself, and now we need to look at the receiver of the gift. We can know all the words to every Christmas carol, send religious Christmas cards, attend every church service or mass that's offered, but the gift of Jesus Christ cannot be truly ours until we choose to believe He is who He says He is and receive Him into our lives.

The most important gift of the season is the one Jesus offers you. If you receive the free gift and invite him into your life you can become a child of God. He said in John 1:12 NIV "To as many as received Him, He gave the right to become cllidren of God."

This shows us that though Jesus offers the gift, until I receive it — until you receive it — we are not fully his. Do you know what this means to you and me? It means that Jesus will not force His way into our lives. He will wait until we choose to invite Him in, to believe in Him and receive him into your life.

Just like the scented candle didn't become_____'s until he (or she) reached out and received it for himself (or herself); Jesus Christ wants each of us to choose to receive him personally.

Church was very important to me as a child and even as a young adult. I knew about the first Christmas and even knew about Easter, but I didn't understand that I needed to choose to believe that Jesus is who He says He is and receive Him into my life. When I realized that, it was like finding the missing piece of a puzzle. (Personalize this paragraph.)

Perhaps there is someone here today who can identify with me. This may be the first time that you have heard that you need to make a choice. You may be silently wondering how to make this choice. We do it simply by expressing to God, through prayer, the desire of our hearts.

In a moment, I am going to pray a simple prayer like I prayed when I received Jesus Christ. I'm going to ask all of us to bow our heads while I pray this simple prayer. If you choose to invite Jesus Christ into your life, just pray along silently with me. Before I pray this prayer, though, I want to say it to you first so you can know what's going to be in it. If this prayer expresses the desire of your heart follow along silently as I pray out loud.

       (Read the prayer thoughtfully and slowly.)

Now, again, if this is the desire of your heart; follow along silently. Let's all bow our heads while I pray.

"Heavenly Father, thank you for sending Your Son, Jesus Christ because You love me so much. I realize for the first time that Jesus died for the sins I have committed, which separate me from You. I want to receive your free gift and invite Jesus to come in and take control of my life. Thank You for coming, into my life. Amen."

If you have prayed a similar prayer before or prayed with me for the first time today, there is a wonderful promise in the Bible that we can cling to in this unstable world. Jesus says, "I will never leave you or forsake you." (Hebrews 13:5 NIV)

For some, Christmas is not a joyful time. Because of deaths of loved ones, broken relationships or moves, many people find Christmas to be a difficult and lonely time. But if Jesus is in your life because you invited him to come in, you have His promise that He will never leave you or forsake you.

When you go home today, this new relationship with Jesus will be very much like the scented candle gift. He will bring a new warm glow to your life and his sweet fragrance will begin to permeate your life very much like this candle will effect _____'s home when he (or she) takes it home and lights it.

Your host has a little gift for you today. When you open it you will see what God wants for Christmas.

      (Give them time to open their compact or family life mirrors.)

Now I want to give all of you the opportunity to communicate how you feel about being here and what has been shared. I have some cards I will pass around. When you're finished filling out your card, please drop it in this basket on the coffee table.

On the card, I'd appreciate your comments on what I shared. If you have any questions, please feel free to share your name and phone number and (host) or I will gladly call you. If you silently prayed along with me and asked Jesus to come in and be the center of your life, would you put "I prayed with you" or an "X" on your card. I will be praying especially this Christmas for those of you who prayed with me tonight. As you return home begin to watch for the changes that knowing Jesus in a real and personal way will make in your life.

(Host) is interested in starting a 4-6 week neighborhood Bible discussion group in January. If you are interested in knowing more about the Bible, please put your name and phone number on the card so you can be contacted when it will begins.

Thank you, (host), for asking me to come and be in your home tonight. I really enjoyed being with you all. I know there is plenty of coffee and goodies left, so help yourself after you've filled out your card, and we'll have more time to visit.

(Play some soft Christmas music for them while they write their cards.)

A Final Suggestion

You may also want to have copies of a booklet for them to take home or to give them on a follow up appointment. An excellent choice is Campus Crusade's pamphlet: "Would You Like to Know God Personally?"

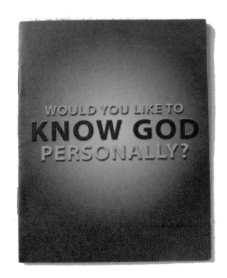

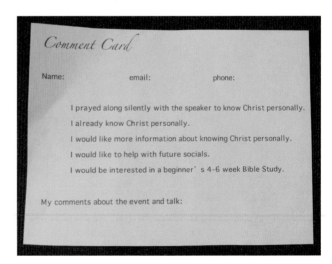

New Year's Celebrations

There are three main types of New Year's Celebrations:

· New Year's Eve party
· New Years Day Brunch
· New Year's Day "Open House"

The evening party can include adults or families. The brunch can be large or small and include all ages. An Open House is a great way to catch up with friends from all your different social contacts. The conversations may be limited since people drop by at various times but it is a nice way to build relationships.

New Year's Day Heavenly Hospitality

Having a New Years event is a great way to build relationships so that you can share the Gospel at a future time. However, if your group is small and conducive to using an ice breaker and a couple of personal stories, feel free to do so. Have people share their New Year's Resolutions or ones that they've made in the past. It could be amusing to hear how they did or did not keep them.

After a time of sharing, have a speaker share the Gospel and name the talk "The Ultimate New Year's Resolution". He or she could give his or her testimony or his or her story about how Jesus changed their life forever.

See chaper 12, pg 186-188 for more information on "Telling Your Story"

Almost any brief, heartfelt changed-life testimony is effective. Maybe you would like to have a couple people share their three minute stories and do a simple "pray with me" to close. Below you will find how to transition into call to commitment prayer which I call the "Pray with Me". Do not be afraid of this part of your event. If you use the suggested quote below it will flow naturally.

Pray with Me

"If what was shared today made sense to you and you would like to start a real and personal relationship with Jesus Christ like _____ _____ has talked about, it is really quite simple. Just tell God that you want to know Jesus Christ personally and open your heart to invite Him in. This is done through prayer and prayer is simply talking to God. He's not so concerned about the words of your prayer as He is about the attitude of your heart. I am going to close our time today with a simple prayer of faith. Follow along silently in your heart, as I pray out loud, if you want to experience the Ultimate New Year's Resolution. Let's pray."

Prayer

"Lord Jesus, I want a real and personal relationship with You like _____ talked about today. I'm not sure how to start, but on this New Year's Day I want to make the ultimate resolution. I open the door of my heart to You. Thank You for dying on the cross for my sins and giving me a new life. Take control of my life and make me the kind of person that You want me to be.
AMEN"

Comment Cards

Perhaps it would be fun to ask guests to write down a New Year's Resolution on a comment card. Refer to the comment card section in the Making Sure of Heaven chapter to fully understand how and why these are effective. Then ask for their thoughts about what the speaker shared. You should plan on following up with those who expressed an interest in accepting Christ. Try the "Questions for God" idea also in Chapter 12.

New Year's Eve Game Night

Many people do not like to be out on the roads on New Year's Eve so inviting families into your home can be a warm safe expression of hospitality. Have your guests arrive around 8:00 PM. Have a variety of board games or large group games depending on the size of the group and the ages involved. If you have space for billiards, ping pong, darts or other such games, have them set up. If you are having eight or more people, you may want to set up several card tables for board games or dominoes and put them on the tables ahead of time.

Keep the refreshments simple. Ask each guest to bring some sort of snack. Have some popcorn popping as your guests arrive. It will make the room smell like a party. Provide a punch bowl which can be replenished throughout the evening as people serve themselves. Liters of soda, ice bucket and glasses on a counter also work. Many people have traditions such as watching TV as the ball drops in Times Square, blowing noise makers and kissing loved ones.

At about 12:10 a.m. turn the TV off and pray a simple blessing for the coming year. This sends a signal to the nonbelievers present that there is something deeper and spiritual about you. You do not want to pray very long because it would make people who are not accustomed to prayer feel uncomfortable. You merely want to close the evening on a positive spiritual note and prayerfully expect further spiritual discussions with your guests at another time and place. By introducing Christian friends to "seekers", you are creating connections for future contact to be made.

Suggested Games

Board Games:	Card Games:	Large Group Games:
Monopoly	Rummy	Pictionary
Life	Hearts	Gestures
Dominoes	Uno	Taboo
Rummikub	Phase 10	Catch Phrase
Risk		Scattergories
Clue		Trivial Pursuit
Stratego	**Tables**	Charades
Sequence	Jigsaw Puzzles (teams can	Who wants to be a Millionaire
Sorry	compete for speed)	Murder Mystery
Parcheesi		Cranium
	Computer/TV games	Loaded Questions
	Wii	True Colors
		Apples to Apples

You're Invited to a
New Year's Eve Game Night!

Bring the whole family
and ring in the new year

Time:

Place:

Dress:

Don't forget to bring:

download this
invitation from
www.Entertaining
ForEternity.com or
copy it from here!

Please RSVP to:

Happy New Year!

You are Invited to a New Year's Day Brunch

Given by:

Address:

Time:

Please RSVP to:

New Year's Eve Prayer

"Lord Jesus, thank you for all the fun we've had together this evening. Thank you for all the blessings of the past year. Now as we look forward to the New Year, go with us and keep us safe and healthy. Bless this New Year for all of us. May it be an extra special year as we journey through it with you." Amen.

download this
invitation from www.
EntertainingForEternity.
com or copy it from here!

New Year's Day Brunch

Set the Tone:

- Do not go over the top. There is no need to even decorate. It's morning, and the day is still young. Keep it simple!
- Create a relaxed atmosphere for yourself and your guests.
- Play relaxed, mellow music or instrumental Praise music

Simplify the Food

Create a warm, leisurely breakfast with pancakes or an easy do-it-yourself cereal bar, plenty of fresh orange juice or blend a smoothie of fresh fruit. Plan ahead and have most everything done the night before.

- Serve your meal buffet style by placing brunch items on a dining room table, sideboard, or kitchen island. Include a stack of lap trays dressed with simple linens and cutlery so guests can serve themselves and find a comfortable place to sit.

- Serve easy egg dishes that you can prepare ahead of time and keep warm in the oven. Add a fruit salad and a basket of warm croissants with jam, or bagels with cream cheese. (Having the food ready to go will take the pressure off you.)
- Get a spiral cut honey ham to serve with rolls if you are having a large crowd.
- Set up a do-it-yourself cereal bar. Offer granolas (with toppings like yogurt and shredded coconut). Buy an assortment of small boxes – single serving size.
- Make pancakes topped with chopped pecans. Warm your maple syrup for a few seconds in the microwave. Have some sliced fresh strawberries and whipped cream on the buffet by the pancakes.
- Create a hot cocoa station with various mixers: espresso shots for mocha, and toffee chips for Liquid Heath bars. Or set up an instant juice bar. Place bowls filled with cut-up fruit next to a juice machine or blender. Make smoothies topped with whipped cream or a sprig of mint.

New Year's (or any time) Open House

Hosting an open house for good friends is an anxiety-free way to welcome the New Year. Start with festive simple decorations. Have finger foods ready on trays ahead of time for your guests to enjoy. A casual buffet of easy, make-ahead foods can be set up in another area. A dessert bar can be an enjoyable station, too. The important thing is to have everything done ahead and ready to serve.

On the invitation be sure to put a beginning and ending time. People can "come and go" as their schedule allows, freeing them up to attend another holiday event. This will also space out the size of your crowd and you can invite more people because not everyone will be there the whole time.

Play upbeat background music, especially at the beginning of the party when there will likely be fewer people at first. Later on when it's the most crowded, you probably won't need music.

Welcome your guests at the front door. Have a tray of beverages nearby to give guests as they arrive. Have "munchies" in the rooms you will be using and replenish the food as needed. Don't forget a light dip and veggies for those who want to eat healthy.

download this invitation from www. EntertainingForEternity. com or copy it from here!

Open House Menu Ideas

- · Mixed Nuts
- · Pretzels and other salty type snacks
- · Chips and Dips
- · Vegetables and Dip
- · Meat balls served in crock pots
- · Cheese and cracker trays
- · Food Club appetizers
- · Mini sandwiches
- · Spiral cut ham with small rolls or croissants
- · Sliced pickles, mustard & mayo
- · Cut-up fruit
- · Bite-size desserts
- · Brownies or Blondies
- · Cookies
- · Cream puffs or éclairs

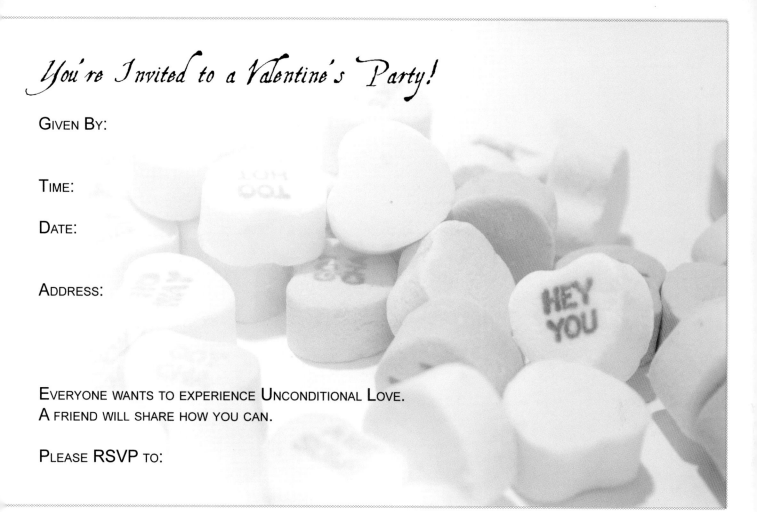

You're Invited to a Valentine's Party!

GIVEN BY:

TIME:

DATE:

ADDRESS:

EVERYONE WANTS TO EXPERIENCE UNCONDITIONAL LOVE.
A FRIEND WILL SHARE HOW YOU CAN.

PLEASE RSVP TO:

Valentine's Day or Couples Event

Valentine's Day lends itself well to events for couples or just ladies. Use the theme of "Unconditional Love." In my last neighborhood, I had a ladies daytime Coffee and asked a friend to speak on putting more romance in our marriages. For the ice breaker we asked the women to share their most romantic or memorable date. My friend spoke about how Christ is the real lover of our souls and explained the basic ideals of Christian marriage.

Couples

One year the women from my Bible Study had a potluck at my house and invited their husbands and a marriage expert to give a talk on Christian marriage. The ladies liked this because many of their husbands did not know the Lord. The men came because they were curious about what their wives were learning and who their new friends were. One of the husbands laughingly told us that he had nicknamed us the "Bible Broads". We all chuckled as we pictured the conversations in their home. We could just imagine what it may have been like as his wife was preparing for our study. He continued to observe us that summer since we had our Bible study around their pool with our kids. He has since come to know Christ personally and it all started with that first exposure at the potluck. An entire family was reached for Christ. The "ABC's of Unconditional Love" handout can be sent home with your guests.

Remember that we need to build trusting relationships with people before we can go into a direct Gospel presentation. Young Life refers to this as "winning the right to be heard".

ABC's of Unconditional Love

God's Valentine to You

A – I accept you as you are

B – I believe you are a valuable person

C – I care for you when you hurt

D – I desire the best for you

E – I erase all of your offenses

"I have loved you with an everlasting love;
I have drawn you with loving kindness."

Jeremiah 31:3b (NIV)

Decorations

Valentine decorations are as easy as it gets. Cut out paper hearts in red, pink and white using the trusty elementary school technique! Fold a small piece of paper in half and cut out half the heart shape (cut the unfolded edge). Place different sized hearts on your table, on counters and elsewhere in the room. Buy some tiny Candy Hearts to use, too.

Valentine Ice Breaker

As your guests arrive, have romantic background music playing softly. Use heart-shaped name tags. On a prominent table, display various romantic and marriage books like:

Men are from Mars, Women are from Venus by Dr. John Gray
1001 Ways to Be Romantic by Gregory J.P. Godek

Invite your guests to sit down with their refreshments and then say,

"Valentine's Day is supposed to be a time set aside for expressing our love and affections to the very special people in your life. We all do this in various ways like giving cards, candy and flowers. Today, before my friend shares, I thought maybe we could help each other out with some fresh ideas. Let's share the most romantic or best date you have been on."

After about 10-15 minutes of sharing, introduce your friend saying:

"Today I have asked my friend, _____ ____, to share something meaningful with us. The title of her talk is How We Can Experience Unconditional Love. These principles have changed the way in which I relate to my loved ones and they work any time of the year."

You will find additional talks on the website

See the Recipe section pg 219 for how to make Corned Beef and Cabbage

St. Patrick's Day

St. Patrick's Day is a celebration in honor of Patrick, Ireland's patron saint. Born in Britain near the end of the 4th Century, Patrick was forced into slavery at age 16 and spent six years herding sheep until he escaped and returned to England. He eventually returned to Ireland as a missionary. Legend says that he used the leaves of a shamrock to explain the meaning of Trinity (the Father, Son, and Holy Spirit). Unfortunately, for many the holiday has turned into an excuse to drink too much, but for "heavenly hospitality" purposes, we can redeem the day by focusing on St. Patrick's love for the Lord. Below is a quote you can print up on decorative green paper. It is in St. Patrick's old Irish style so break it down and use it to explain the Gospel to your guests. Make enough copies so that everyone can go home with one.

Saint Patrick's Day decorations are simple -- shamrocks and lots of green. Coffees or Desserts can be as simple as shamrock cookies or white cake with green icing. Serve Irish Cream flavored creamers with dollops of whipped cream. Teas could include butter cookies in the shape of shamrocks and cucumber and egg salad tea sandwiches. Have some neighbors in for corned beef and cabbage (easy crock pot or oven meal) served with Irish soda bread from the bakery. You can read more about this interesting holiday online or at the library.

"So that whatever befalls me, be it good or bad, I should accept it equally, and give thanks always to God, who revealed to me that I might trust in him, implicitly and forever, and who will encourage me so that, ignorant, and in the last days, I may dare to undertake so devout and so wonderful a work; so that I might imitate one of those whom, once, long ago, the Lord already preordained to be heralds of his Gospel to witness to all peoples to the ends of the earth."
St Patrick of Ireland

Chapter 8

My mother used to tell me we knew it was springtime when the first robin appeared. It's probably different for each part of the country, but Spring conjures up a new beginning for just about all of us. It officially begins on March 21st. Ask the Lord to help you think of creative ways to use any of the following occasions to show some Heavenly Hospitality to those around you. Be sure to check our web site for updated new ideas. Since it's the time of year when everything is coming to life, it makes a perfect introduction for the Gospel message. The Butterfly Spring talk, provided below can be used at many times during Spring.

Spring Days to celebrate:

- First Day of Spring (March 21st) *
- Passover -
  explain how Jesus is our Passover Lamb
- Easter *
- Earth Day (April 22nd) *
- May Day (1st)
- Mother's Day and Father's Day
- Cinco de Mayo (May 5th)

* These are occasions where the "Butterfly Talk" on pg 139 can be used.

Spring or Easter Event

After a dreary winter, everyone is open to a party. Their social calendar is still a little slow and the busy, outdoor days are still ahead. You can celebrate Spring on its first day, March 21st or wait until Easter and plan an informative event.

There are two times of year we never have to apologize for talking about Jesus: Easter and Christmas. They are our holidays and often un-churched people are curious about them so make the most of them!

Another Easter idea is to have a video party where you invite people into your home to watch the Jesus video produced by The Jesus Film Project. If children come, show the children's version and try ending it with an Easter egg hunt. For a children's party see that section of this manual.

To secure the videos or DVDs contact: The JESUS Film Project/Video Department at 1800-492-0381 or www.jesusforchildren.org

Often our family will invite an un-churched couple or family to join us for Easter. We let the pastor's sermon be the "direct" evangelism. We invite them to our church service and to our home for a traditional Easter dinner. There are still some "Twice a Year Church People" out there who would love to go to church on Easter as well as Christmas but don't know where to go or are hesitant. An invitation to join your family may be just what they need. George Barna, the Christian pollster, says that one out of four Americans say that they would attend a church event or service if someone would invite them. That's 15-18 million Americans just waiting to be asked!

Spring or Easter Coffee or Dessert

A tradition we have used at Easter is a special Holy Week Basket. Each person takes an item from the basket and the card that goes with that item. Each card is read in the correct order and the item is held up for all to see. My husband says a brief blessing for the meal. Children love handling and showing their item from the basket.

If you can find a huge spike to put in your basket for the Good Friday card, it can have a powerful effect. I have one that I wrote this quote on, "I did this for you." Sometimes we forgo reading the cards from the basket and just pass it around the table before the blessing so that each person can handle the items in it and the Holy Spirit can speak to them silently.

When little children are present, we try to end with an Easter egg hunt. Another excellent idea for children is to use "Resurrection Eggs" either at the dinner table or just before the hunt. The eggs can be ordered from www.familylifetoday.org.

Holy Week Basket Cards

Paste the verses on the following pages to 3x5 cards and place in a basket with the following items:
1. Palm branch
2. Small sample size of perfume
3. A plastic communion cup and saltine or matzo cracker
4. A small circle of rose bush branches
5. A large nail and small homemade wooden cross
6. A strip of white cloth
7. A large stone

Pass the basket around your table before serving Easter dinner. Have each guest take a card and the appropriate item that goes with their card. Then have the guests read their card and show their item. Read the cards in their numerical order. Children especially enjoy this.

Or use the basket with your family during Easter/Holy Week. Start on Monday and read card #1 and continue each night through Holy Week ending with the stone on Easter Sunday.

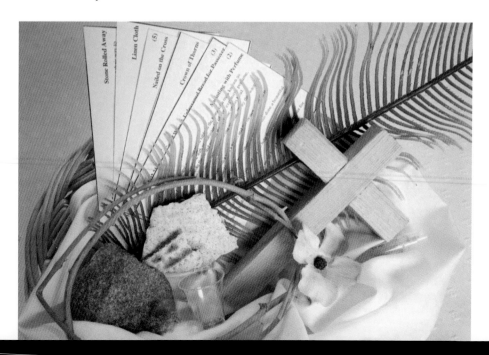

1. Mark 11:7-10 NIV   Palm Sunday

When they brought the colt to Jesus and threw their cloaks over it, he
sat on it. Many people spread their cloaks on the road, while others
spread branches they had cut in the fields. Those who went ahead and
those who followed shouted, "Hosanna!" "Blessed is he who comes in
the name of the Lord!" "Blessed is the coming kingdom of our father
David!" "Hosanna in the highest!"

2. Mark 14:3-8 NIV   Anointing with Perfume

While he was in Bethany, reclining at the table in the home of a man
known as Simon the Leper, a woman came with an alabaster jar of very
expensive perfume, made of pure nard. She broke the jar and poured
the perfume on his head.

Some of those present were saying indignantly to one another, "Why
this waste of perfume? It could have been sold for more than a year's
wages and the money given to the poor." And they rebuked her harshly.
"Leave her alone," said Jesus. "Why are you bothering her? She has
done a beautiful thing to me. The poor you will always have with you,
and you can help them any time you want. But you will not always
have me. She did what she could. She poured perfume on my body
beforehand to prepare for my burial.

3. Mark 14:12-15, 22-24 NIV
                      Cup of Wine & Unleavened Bread for Passover

On the first day of the Feast of Unleavened Bread, when it was customary
to sacrifice the Passover lamb, Jesus' disciples asked him, "Where do you
want us to go and make preparations for you to eat the Passover?" So he
sent two of his disciples, telling them, "Go into the city, and a man carrying
a jar of water will meet you. Follow him. Say to the owner of the house he
enters, 'The Teacher asks: Where is my guest room, where I may eat the
Passover with my disciples?' He will show you a large upper room, furnished
and ready. Make preparations for us there."

While they were eating, Jesus took bread, gave thanks and broke it, and
gave it to his disciples, saying, "Take it; this is my body." Then he took the
cup, gave thanks and offered it to them, and they all drank from it. "This is
my blood of the covenant, which is poured out for many," he said to them.

4. Mark 15:17-20 NIV   Crown of Thorns

They put a purple robe on him, then twisted together a crown of thorns
and set it on him. And they began to call out to him, "Hail, king of the
Jews!" Again and again they struck him on the head with a staff and
spit on him. Falling on their knees, they paid homage to him. And when
they had mocked him, they took off the purple robe and put his own
clothes on him. Then they led him out to crucify him.

5. Mark 15:24-28, 39 NIV   Nailed on the Cross

And they crucified him. Dividing up his clothes, they cast lots to see
what each would get.

It was the third hour when they crucified him. The written notice of
the charge against him read: the king of the jews. They crucified two
robbers with him, one on his right and one on his left.

And when the centurion, who stood there in front of Jesus, heard his
cry and saw how he died, he said, "Surely this man was the Son of
God!"

6. Mark 15:44-46 NIV   Linen Cloth

Pilate was surprised to hear that he was already dead. Summoning the
centurion, he asked him if Jesus had already died. When he learned
from the centurion that it was so, he gave the body to Joseph. So
Joseph bought some linen cloth, took down the body, wrapped it in the
linen, and placed it in a tomb cut out of rock. Then he rolled a stone
against the entrance of the tomb.

You're Invited to come Celebrate Easter with us!

Given by:

When:

Where:

Please RSVP to:

download this invitation from www.Entertaining ForEternity.com and print them or copy it straight from here!

7. Mark 16:2-6 NIV   Stone Rolled Away

Very early on the first day of the week, just after sunrise, they were on their way to the tomb and they asked each other, "Who will roll the stone away from the entrance of the tomb?" But when they looked up, they saw that the stone, which was very large, had been rolled away. As they entered the tomb, they saw a young man dressed in a white robe sitting on the right side, and they were alarmed. "Don't be alarmed," he said. "You are looking for Jesus the Nazarene, who was crucified. He has risen! He is not here. See the place where they laid him.

Come Celebrate Spring!

given by:

address:

time:

place:

a friend will be sharing some
inspirational thoughts about the season

please RSVP to:

Speaker's Introduction:

"I love the way all of nature seems to come alive and is new and fresh every Spring. Recently, a friend sent me an email that I'd like to share with you. Before __(speaker)__ comes. It's a story about a springtime butterfly.

Butterfly Illustration

A man found a cocoon of a butterfly. One day, a small opening appeared. He sat and watched the butterfly for several hours as it struggled to force its body through that little hole. Then it seemed to stop making any progress. It appeared as if it had gotten as far as it could, and it could go no further. So the man decided to help the butterfly. He took a pair of scissors, and snipped off the remaining bit of the cocoon. The butterfly then emerged easily. But it had a swollen body and small, shriveled wings. The man continued to watch the butterfly because he expected that at any moment the wings would enlarge and expand to be able to support the body, which would contract in time. Neither happened! In fact, the butterfly spent the rest of its life crawling around with a swollen body and shriveled wings. It never was able to fly. What the man, in his kindness and haste did not understand, was that the restricting cocoon and struggle required for the butterfly to get through the tiny opening were God's way of forcing fluid from the body of the butterfly into its wings so that it would be ready for flight once it achieved its freedom from the cocoon.

Sometimes, struggles are exactly what we need in our lives. If God allowed us to go through our lives without any obstacles, it would cripple us. We would not be as strong as what we could have been. We could never fly!

author unknown

This can be read by the host or by the speaker as the opening part of their talk. It could also be printed on Spring-themed paper with butterfly designs. It makes a great piece for guests to take home. I often have people ask me for a copy.

Patriotic Picnics

A few years ago, we decided to initiate an annual neighborhood picnic. Everyone loves a cookout and it can be easy if you elect to have a potluck. The host provides the meats on the grill, makes the iced tea and lemonade and asks everyone to bring a salad or dessert. Assigning guests to bring something allows them also to take "ownership" of the event. Generally, these picnics are in the "relational" category where the main goal is to develop relationships with people you would like to introduce to Christ. The only thing spiritual that you should do is to give a blessing or prayer before they go through the food line. This will show your friends that there is something deeper going on in your life. You want to make them curious because the Bible says that we should be "salt and light" in our world.

Patriotic picnics can be held on almost any national holiday: Fourth of July, Memorial Day, Flag Day or Labor Day. Take the opportunity to pray for our nation and for our president in your blessing before the meal. If our country is going through a difficult time, include that in your prayer. Very few people will complain if you include this type of prayer in your event.

After you get everyone's attention and give the directions for the food line, say something like this;

> "It's our custom in our home to say a simple blessing before we eat our meals. Would you please join me as I ask God to bless our food and our country?"   (Pause and then pray)

Prayer

"Dear Lord, thank you for our wonderful country and the freedoms that we enjoy. Help us to never take them for granted. Thank you for friends and this wonderful food that you have blessed us with. Grant us rich conversations and a fun time this afternoon. Amen"

Worried About Offending?

If you think something like this will offend your neighbors, don't worry. Our neighbors have even proposed at our Homeowners Annual Meeting that we continue the picnics as a regular neighborhood tradition.

Decorations

Have fun decorating the tables in red, white and blue. Purchase some small American flags and put them in flower pots or planters. Wear a flag shirt or something red, white and blue. Buy flags early before the stores are sold out! Put them all over the yard or deck, and in centerpieces. String some white twinkling lights around, too.

Food

Shopping list:
- Frozen burger patties
- Hot dogs
- Buns
- Condiments: Catsup, relish, mustard, sliced tomatoes and onions

Since it's a potluck, all you have to do is grill the hamburgers and hotdogs. When people R.S.V.P. ask them what they plan to bring. To bring out the theme serve strawberries, blueberries and whip cream. How easy is that? If you want to get fancy, layer them in clear glasses or top a sheet cake with them.

YOU'RE INVITED!

**Come celebrate American
Independence, Patriotism and Freedom!**

DATE: ....

TIME: ....

LOCATION:
....

....

**Wear red, white and blue clothing and
bring an American potluck dish to share.**

*Patriotic Picnic
Invitation*

You can download the invite to
print from the website www.
EntertainingForEternity.com

Fourth of July Ideas

Red-blooded Americans love to celebrate the Fourth of July. You can have a simple potluck picnic with burgers and hotdogs on the backyard grill, and have sparklers and fireworks. (Fireworks may be prohibited in your area so check the rules). Be the one in your neighborhood to start a traditional block party on one of the patriotic holidays. Don't forget to invite Internationals to join you to learn more about our country. They are curious about our country and love being included. Consider going as a group to a local fireworks display. Play traditional backyard games like:

- Three legged races
- Balloon stomps or toss
- Horseshoes
- Badminton
- Croquet
- Wiffle ball
- Capture the Flag
- Patriotic Pictionary:
    Teams race to draw and identify the following words: George Washington, White House, Abraham Lincoln, The Capital, Betsy Ross, The Star-Spangled Banner; the Liberty Bell; The Boston Tea Party, God Bless America, Yankee Doodle.

Dessert on the Deck or Pastries on the Patio

A very simple way to connect with your neighbors is to invite your neighbors over for an informal time to get to know each other better. Plan it at the beginning of the outdoor season, although anytime will work. Serve simple desserts and provide pots of coffee or pitchers of iced tea.

Desserts on the deck

time:
date:
location:

come relax with us and satisfy your sweet tooth!

please RSVP to:

Copy this invite from here or download this invite from www.EntertainingFor Eternity.com

Chapter 10

Couples and Men's Only Events

There's nothing more powerful or thrilling than seeing a couple come to Christ and a whole new family transformed for all Eternity. Reach out to the couples you know from work; your neighborhood, clubs or associations, and sports; as well as those you know through your children. Look for ways to include the husbands of the women in your social circles. Quite often, it's the wife who comes to Christ first.

One evening as we were leaving our ballroom dance class, we invited another couple to join us for a bite to eat. We enjoyed talking to them about our travels since becoming empty-nesters. In the course of one hour we learned they loved to travel as much as we did. One trip of ours was especially intriguing to them, it was a mission trip to Ethiopia. I surprised myself by blurting out, "You ought to go on a mission trip; that is how you really get to see the country. Do

you have a church? Maybe they run some mission trips." The wife responded, "I used to have a church." Then, the husband chirped in with "Wow! Not only would you get to travel, but you'd actually do something good too!" They were leaving on a sailing trip to the Caribbean and we told them to be sure to take lots of pictures, we'd want to see them when they got home. We left with new friends in whom we were genuinely interested.

We continue to see them at our ballroom dance classes, and hope the relationship will grow and that they will eventually begin to ask us more questions about the spiritual aspect of our lives. By the time you are reading this book, this couple may have come to know Christ personally simply because we asked them to join us for a salad. That's how easy it is to Entertain for Eternity with Heavenly Hospitality.

I could fill a book with stories like this and their happy endings. One of the most ironic is from our neighborhood in Pennsylvania. As was our custom, we had started a small, couple's Bible Study. A new couple moved in behind us so we invited them to our group. We were all happy when they came the very next week! They told the group that they had just been to a palm reader who had suggested that they do something to develop their spiritual life – and the next day they were invited to come to our Bible study! Thinking that this was what the palm reader meant, they came! I can happily tell you that this couple went on to fully trust Christ with their lives and went on to grow in their faith. They have joined a church where the husband is an elder and they have traveled on several mission trips.

You never know what's going on in other people's lives that is preparing them for your invitation. Don't be shy and hesitant. You may miss out on the blessing of seeing God work through you. We have seen God do similar things time after time. Stories like this encourage us to believe God will do the same sorts of things with other couples and I hope they will encourage you to try some of the ideas in this chapter. There's a world of lonely couples just waiting for an invitation!

New Neighbors

Reach out to new couples when they first move into your neighborhood. When a family is going through a major change, they are most open. On moving day, take them a loaf of bread from a bakery and give them information about the neighborhood or local shopping areas. Give them your phone number in case they have any questions or you can help in any way. I can't tell you how many times neighbors have come back later and told us that we were the only ones to greet them, or how much our visit meant to them.

Military Families

Military families say that quite often other families do not bother to reach out to them because they know that they are probably going to move in a couple of years. They are lonely and quite often do not have family nearby. Include them in your family holidays.

Internationals

Do not hesitate to entertain people from other countries. Ask questions, learn about them and build relationships. Everyone just wants to know that someone else cares. They are curious about Americans and American traditions. Invite them for any holiday. A patriotic picnic or Thanksgiving is a good one to start with. Your children will learn about different parts of the world from entertaining international guests.

Some German friends were fascinated by our Thanksgiving dinner. They had many questions about our holidays and our families became life-time friends. One Christmas we were able to give them a copy of the Jesus Film in their own language. We even stayed with them on a recent mission's trip. What fun it was to see and experience the real Germany, riding bikes through farm fields to the local bakery to buy fresh breakfast rolls. We felt at home with them, not like regular tourists in Germany.

Your Church Small Group

Get your couples group to do an event from this book as an outreach to your community. Use the Bible discussion at the end of the book with your small group to motivate them to do an event.

What to Say or Do

You are probably wondering now, "What do we say? What do we do when these couples come over?" Use any of the holiday ideas in each of the previous chapters. If it's not a holiday; have them over for no special reason at all. Choose some conversation stimulators from this chapter that you feel comfortable with. Commit them to memory or write them on slips of paper. Put them in a bowl and let guests choose one. Play games like the ones listed in the New Years Eve section. Watch a movie like "The Story of Us" and discuss what we can learn about our marriages from this or what can we learn about our parenting. Be a good listener. Do not correct them but wait for their questions about your family.

Introverts

A young friend in her mid 20's confided to me that one thing that holds her back from having people over is her fear of not knowing what to say. She is a true introvert. Many people are! I like to think that I'm a converted introvert. My kindergarten teacher wrote a note to my parents. She said that she was worried about me because I rarely talked and played all alone. Somewhere over the years I've gotten over that. Perhaps going into ministry forced me to develop this area of my life, too. However, I can still easily identify with the apostle Paul in 1 Corinthians 2:1-5 (NIV) when he said that he came to them "with fear and trembling" and not using lofty words (verse 3). Even extroverts can use a little help directing conversations into meaningful interactions that will have eternal rewards.

You will find the "conversation stimulators" in this book and on the web site very helpful. Do not be afraid of silences. Give guests time to think. This may be the very first time that they've tried to express themselves on these topics. Everyone appreciates it when you care enough to listen to what they think and how they feel. We live in a world of disconnected or isolated people. They need to know someone cares about them.

One Secular Couple's Story

I was surprised to find this truth in the October, 2002 issue of Better Homes and Garden Magazine. It was an article about a young secular couple in their late 20's who began inviting all sorts of people to come to their home for dinner to try out recipes. Their simple family suppers became so popular that neighbors began coming up to them in the street asking to be included. They served as many as 20 people on a make-shift tables made from doors and saw horses. The price of admission was a chair or a plate and maybe a few dollars to cover expenses.

They said, "Conversation sparkled and strangers became family over the course of an evening. To keep the gathering fresh, each guest was required to bring a newcomer." The couple went on to say, "Feeding people means more than just nourishing bodies. It's about nourishing souls. I hope they feel taken care of in a really different way - supported. The dinners seem to get people talking about what they would do if they could do anything. Are you doing what you want to be doing with your life? We aren't shy about encouraging people to look at that."

If secular people can invite neighbors over for a meal, it gives great credibility to the fact that it's okay to approach unbelievers with "conversation stimulators".

Willow Creek Seeker Parties

Willow Creek Church near Chicago, Illinois is a mega-church that is doing what I'm suggesting to you. They call them "Seeker Parties". Here's what their pastor, Bill Hybels, said to the congregation in an email one day.

"Last night Lynne and I hosted a small "seeker party". Having done lots of these over the years we know that sometimes something supernatural happens and other times we have to settle for just sowing seeds that may germinate at a later date. Last night was one of those evenings when the least likely people to open up did. If I live to be a hundred, I will never tire of watching the Spirit do His work in those moments when eternity is literally hanging in the balance. I could barely sleep last night. Friends, if you have never hosted a seeker dinner, plan one soon. Take the risk. Who knows what God might do!"

Much like the young couple in the Better Homes and Gardens magazine article, "conversation stimulators" take your event to a deeper more meaningful and more memorable level. These occasions can be either:

- Relational: building relationships for a future Gospel presentation
- Invitational: includes a full Gospel presentation

The Evangelistic Gospel presentation can come in several forms:

- Prepared program: a movie, concert, TV show or webcast.
- Testimonial message: where one or more believers share their story
- Speaker: gives a prepared talk based on a topic or holiday, etc.

Relational events can occur any time you gather together to get to know people better and build a relationship with them. Sometime you will do what I call "tip your hat". That means you'll give just a hint that there is a spiritual dimension to you and your family. Sometimes that is merely saying a short simple grace before you eat. You do not say anything unless it comes up naturally. Build a caring relationship and wait until they ask for more information. If it doesn't come right away, that's okay. Continue to be their friend. Reach out to them and help where you can. As time goes by give a bigger hint and wait. When you feel like you are genuine friends and that the Holy Spirit is prompting, take your conversations to a more spiritual level by inviting them to something with a Gospel presentation. If the event is at your home, remember not to be the speaker. Afterwards, ask them the three post-event questions on the following page. They will be more honest with you because you were not the speaker.

3 Post-Event Questions

- What did you think of the talk?
- Did the talk make sense?
- Would you like to know more about the speaker's topic?
(Make sure you say this with expectancy in your voice.)

Invitational Event Ideas

- Watch events on TV such as bowl games, the Oscars or a video
- Cookouts
- Walk together in the neighborhood
- Game night for couples
- Have couples bring their wedding albums and sharing how they first met or what their first date was like

For Men Only

Women are usually considered to be more social than men but for some couples, that's not always the case. Women are usually the keepers of the family social schedule, but that does not let men off the hook. With so many women working outside the home, more men are helping out at home and have more domestic skills than their fathers ever did. When the family is entertaining and showing hospitality, all too often men think all that they have to do is show up. NOT SO! Single and married men can do or help with any of the events in this book.

My husband has the "gift of helps" so he's always been very involved when we have people in our home. Also, his parents modeled Entertaining for Eternity with Heavenly Hospitality. But even he can get busy with his own agenda and come rushing in the door just before guests arrive. In the movie "Breaking Up," Jennifer Aniston is busily preparing for dinner guests. Her partner comes in from work, throws on his casual clothes, and flops on the couch, oblivious to her need in the kitchen. Sadly, it's all too common. The irony in this situation is that the guests are his friends and relatives. The drama that follows is sad and far too typical.

Quite often a man wants to have the "guys" over for a pickup basketball game or watch one on TV. He may want to invite some people from his office over for dinner. He needs to own the event and get involved. When we worked with students, sometimes Sam would phone home and ask if someone could come home for dinner. Many times I put "another bean in the pot" and the Lord did the "fish and loaves trick" again. Sam always pitched in and helped. We had an open-door policy with the students and when we worked at a Campus Crusade for Christ beach project one summer, there was one lifeguard who regularly showed up at our at dinnertime looking forlorn. He and Sam did the dishes while they talked. Informal discipleship took place.

The best thing a man can do is to know the overall event plan and ask how he can help and be involved. There are little jobs that even the most undomesticated man can do. If he looks around, he can anticipate the needs of the hour. It is important for him to take the lead spiritually for the event. Pray together before your guests arrive. Learn and use some conversation stimulators that he feels comfortable with. Men can offer the meal time prayer. Show that being spiritual is not only a female thing; demonstrate that it's manly to lead spiritually.

Helpful Participation can mean little things like:

- Vacuum and help pick up around the house
- Fill water glasses
- Light candles and choose background music
- Serve the appetizer beverages
- Build a fire in the fireplace or grill
- Grill the meat
- Give the bathroom a quick wipe-up
- Make sure the kids are clean and in a cheerful mood
- Greet the guests at the door
- Hang up coats
- Prepare the nametags for a large event.
- Clear the table
- Serve the coffee

Men's Events

Some events are for men only. Men can do Entertaining for Eternity with Heavenly Hospitality in a variety of settings. Check the website for more ideas to get more ideas for men's events. Recently a friend was telling me he had a men's open house which he called an "Open Truck". His humorous story is on the website. Check it out!

Dad's Dessert

A friend of mine had an outreach ministry that he called "Dad's Dessert." He served homemade, upscale desserts -- no box mixes. If the recipe called for whipped cream it was real whipped cream! These meetings were held on the first Monday of the month between October through May and he did this for ten years! Guests had to be a dad or an expectant dad. Dessert was first followed by what he called "Sharp Focus" where he would lead the men in discussions on topics related to fatherhood. After the presentation and discussion the guys could hang around for Monday night football or whatever playoff game was on television. Most stayed for only the first half of the game because of work the next day. Usually there were 10 to 25 guys sprawled all over his living room.

During the Sharp Focus time they discussed such topics as handling money, teaching kids about money, the spiritual needs of children, etc. Most of the time his wife wasn't even home – it was his turn at Entertaining for Eternity. One year the guys even compiled a cook book of their favorite desserts.

Single working men can be creative when it comes to entertaining. So many grocery stores and restaurants have some pretty fabulous takeout meals. Who can't bake a large frozen lasagna and get a salad from their salad bar? Grab a loaf of bread on your way past the bakery department. Ice cream is always a welcome dessert.

Moving Day Party

If you are moving out of your home or apartment, plan a party and invite your friends to come over. Tell them to bring cleaning supplies, lawn chairs or a blanket to sit on and coolers full of water and soda. The coolers make wonderful seats as well! You can have a potluck dinner, a barbeque or order pizza.

Most movers will not move paint, flammable materials, cleaning products, charcoal, etc., so we share a meal, and then we clean and divide up the items the movers will not take. You can also help neighbors who are moving away. Pray with them before they leave. Farewells are bittersweet, but sharing your last day with those you have grown to love is a great blessing!

We have also done the reverse and had a Move-In Day party. With lots of hands, the hauling of furniture and boxes goes quickly. Take a picnic to new neighbors and get to know them.

Home-Builders (Couples Groups)

Hosting and leading a small group of married couples in your home for an evening can help develop and strengthen Christian marriages. The Family Life "Home-Builders Couples Series" does a wonderful job developing small group biblically based materials for couples to use to strengthen their marriages, develop supportive relationships with other couples and have fun!

Our friends Dana and Steve had 8 couples in a group;t with marriages ranging from 12 weeks to 31 years! The more seasoned couples are being used to mentor the younger marriages. God is doing a transforming work each week in the lives of both individuals and couples. To obtain this series go to www.familylifetoday.com

Men can also show hospitality by helping someone with yard work or shoveling snow. My husband has pleased many neighbors that way. One time he helped a neighbor woman quickly repair the damaged molding around her garage door before her husband came home. Too bad he couldn't fix her car! Keep your eye out for the elderly or someone who is sick. Some other hospitable things could be:

- Clean gutters for elderly
- Drive a shut-in somewhere
- Help with computers
- Fix a flat tire

Chapter 11

Children's Events

> Jesus said, "Let the little children come to me.
> Do not keep them away.
> For of such is the Kingdom of Heaven.
> Matthew 19:14 NIV

It is easy to overlook showing Heavenly Hospitality to children but I think they are our most important guests. Not only are they the easiest group to please, they are our future. If you reach a child for Christ, you tap directly into a family. Hopefully the whole family will come to Christ. Children are easy because they do not notice a messy house and do not care how fancy the food is. All they care about is that someone loves them and thinks they are special.

It is so simple to bring children's entertaining into your life. Have your home child-friendly with a stash of books, games and toys available, then tell your children that their friends are always welcome in your home. Invite neighbor kids to Vacation Bible School or other church programs. Have them over to make cookies, cupcakes, to play games or simply "hang out". Take advantage of occasions to dye Easter eggs, relax after ball games, or enjoy some popcorn and a cup of hot chocolate after sledding. Maybe consider starting a Sunday night youth group. If your home is always open to your children's friends, you will know where your kids are, who they are associating with, and how to know their friends better!

As a child, I experienced Heavenly Hospitality

I came to faith in Christ because a family down the street showed me Heavenly Hospitality. I loved being in their home even though none of their kids were my age. I thought their mom was "cool". (She even went snow sledding with the kids.) She always made me feel special and welcome. I would often stay for a meal or just "hang out" at their house. Other neighborhood kids did, too. What was it about that family that was so attractive to me? It was the warmth that radiated from them because they knew and loved the Lord. I came away from being with them thinking, "That's the kind of home I want when I grow up." You may have no idea what an impact you could have on the children in your neighborhood.

When I was only 9 years old the same family hosted a Child Evangelism Good News Club. It was very simple: a flannelgraph story, a craft and verse along with a song or two. All the hostess-mom did was open her front door and put out a plate of cookies. The CEF staff woman did everything else.

I will always remember the story about the broad and narrow roads. I can still see the flannelgraph images of the broad road

Go to Child Evangelism's web site for more info: www. cefonline.com. They offer kits in English and Spanish which include everything you need to start a club: story, games, craft ideas which can be ordered on line.

leading to fire and the narrow road leading to a cloud with Jesus on it. The little old lady who told the story said that if any child wanted to know for sure that they were going to heaven, they should stay after the club and she would explain how.

Of course I wanted to go to heaven! Who wouldn't? The Wordless Book produced by Child Evangelism said the streets were paved with gold! (This booklet can be obtained from their web site.) A handful of us stayed after the club that day and learned how we could be sure of heaven. She told us it was by asking Jesus Christ into our lives. Even though I was only 9, I can still remember the couch where I knelt as I prayed and gave my life to Jesus Christ.

I'm sure that hostess had no idea how her Heavenly Hospitality that day was going to affect all of Eternity. Little did she know that the little girl kneeling at her couch would go on to serve the Lord in Christian work. That little girl would not only lead her whole family to Christ but spend many years on campuses leading students to the Lord. What's more, that nine-year-old girl grew up to have a ministry to wives of Congressmen, Senators and Governors.

Who knows? You may even have the next Billy Graham, Luis Palau, Kay Arthur or Beth Moore living down the street in your neighborhood. So open your front door to the children on your street.

Important Facts about Children

- 30% of the world's population is under age 15
- By 2010 half the world will be under age 18
- 80% of children live in non-Christian or unchurched homes
- 85% of all Christians came to faith before age 14

Benefits of Heavenly Hospitality to Children

- It uses our homes in a non-threatening environment to glorify God by bringing children to Christ.
- It's an easy and simple way to share Christ clearly with many children at one time.
- It builds relationships in a fractured world.
- It counteracts the isolation and cocooning of our culture. (Many children are never invited into someone's home.)
- It has the potential to reach not only the children but also entire families for Christ.

Ideas to Try with Children

- Load neighborhood kids in your car on Sunday mornings for Sunday School
- Drop off a carload of kids at your church for Daily Vacation Bible School, AWANAs or Youth Groups
- Invite children in to watch Christian DVD's after school.
- Show The Story of Jesus for Children at Christmas or Easter. (See ideas later in this chapter and at www.jesusforchildren.org)

Singles and Empty Nesters

You may think that you have to be married with children to show hospitality to them. Not true! Often children will warm up to singles more quickly than to preoccupied parents. Have an event for the children in your apartment complex or neighborhood. Have a mom join you to help. She will be known by the other moms and give credibility to your event. The mom can help you with the discipline and you come off as the fun single! Neighborhood moms have continuing contact with the children. Use the community room or the playground. Contact CEF and they will provide a teacher to help you.

I had a Child Evangelism summer 5 Day Club when my own kids were grown. My daughter, Kristi, was working one summer for CEF so I had her do the teaching. All I had to do was phone around the neighborhood and invite the children. I made instant lemonade and cookies or some simple snacks. Kristi did all the hard work. The moms on my street were really appreciative and several of the kids asked the Lord into their lives. I still have a special relationship with those families to this day.

Tips for Singles or People who do not children at home

- Singles are loved by children
- Build a relationship with the children on your block or in your complex
- Ask a neighborhood mom to come to your event
- Have your event in the park, playground, or community room.

Having sit-down family dinners

- gives the parents insight to their children's feelings and perceptions
- helps children learn how to express themselves
- teaches them to listen and appreciate others
- allows them to learn about their parents' day and what's important to them
- builds a strong, caring family.

My friend, Debbie, had family dinners every night. Neighborhood kids were often at her table. One night her children asked if a neighbor boy could stay for dinner. Of course the answer was, "Yes." The noisy children gathered around the kitchen table for the simple family supper. As usual they all took hands, bowed their heads, as the father said the grace. As soon as the "Amen" was pronounced and the little heads looked up, the visiting child declared, "Wow! Just like the Waltons!" He had never seen a traditional family meal.

One time, when my college son had a buddy over, they were rushing around to leave for an outing. I persuaded them to hang on for a few minutes since dinner was almost ready and they would save money eating at home. As was our tradition we began the meal with a short word of prayer and during the dessert, before the boys left, my husband read a page out of the "Daily Bread" devotional. My son's friend began to open up and share his thoughts. He was so appreciative of being included that he thanked us genuinely. He asked us if we did that every night and we assured him that we did. He went on to say that his family never ate together. As we queried further, we learned that his family members basically fended for themselves.

Meal Ideas to Try

Invite a family with 3 or 4 kids for a kid-friendly meal and games. (They almost never get invitations because of the sheer size of their family.)

Show Heavenly Hospitality by making meals for families:
- when they are new to the neighborhood, particularly on move-in day
- after a new baby's arrival
- when there is illness or death in the family.

They came in when they were hungry and grazed through the kitchen looking for whatever suited them. They took what they had foraged and ate in front of the TV alone or with whomever else was around. I'm afraid that is what too many American families are still doing!

Our daughter Kristi and her husband, Darrin, have started a family dinner tradition of their own. Kristi, Darrin, and our granddaughter, Lily, have always had family sit down meals. Every night at dinner they talk about their day by having each person share their "High" and "Low" for the day. It's so much fun to listen to Lily and what she shares!

Benefits to your Children

- Models gracious hospitality
- Teaches them manners
- Develops family traditions
- Trains them for their future home
- Provides a place to be nurtured, feel safe, re-group and re-fuel.

Planning a Children's Event

- Pick a theme or holiday. Refer back to the adult chapters for ideas or check the web sites such as familyfun.com, CEFonline.com, or onceuponafamily.com
- Pick date and specify starting and ending times
- Determine the content or program (DVD, read a story, CEF program, etc.)
- Plan an activity, game or craft
- Decide on refreshments
- Determine who to invite

Invitations

An important part of the invitation is to include an ending time. Otherwise, you may find yourself with extra children hanging around long after the party was meant to be over. Parents may stay out shopping or enjoying their freedom and stay away too long for you and your family. Some sample invitations are given on the website for you to print out on your computer. It's nice to have something to put on the refrigerator to remind your family of the upcoming children's event. You might want to call each child to remind them of the event. Use the "Age plus 1" rule for determining how many children to invite.   For example, if your child is only 4 years old then invite only 5 children to your party. If your child is 7 then invite 8 children. If they are 10, invite 11 and so on. Also, consider the amount of room or space you have to accommodate the children. Put away delicate knick-knacks if you are concerned that something might possibly be in the way or get broken.

EASY

Event Essentials for Children

E = Excitedly greet, welcome and introduce the children all around.

A = Any Activity is fun: game or craft

S = Simple Stories read or watched

Y = Yummy snack and You!

Age Groups

After trying several different children's parties with friends, we have determined that they usually need to be arranged by age groups. It's not sensible to group children as young as 4 years old with those who are a great deal older. From what we have observed, however, four different age groups seem to work well.

- Ages 4 – 6 years old
- Grades 1 – 3
- Grades 4 – 6
- Grades 7 – 8 (add 9th grade if it is included in your local junior high school)

Story Books that make a great children's event feature

- The Christmas Lizard by Cory Edwards
- The Crippled Lamb by Max Lucado
- The Legend of The Three Trees by Catherine McCafferty
- The Easter Story by Cathy Ann Johnson
- Squanto and the Miracle of Thanksgiving by Eric Metaxas
- The Candy Maker's Gift by David and Helen Haidle
- What God Wants for Christmas by Amy L. Bradford

Older Children

The size of your house does not matter! My friend Cathy has an open door policy at her home, young people are always welcome. She told me this story:

"When our son, Tommy, was at Messiah College, he wanted to bring his close knit group of friends home for the weekend -- about 20 some guys and gals. He knew our old house was not big, not fancy, no dishwasher, not at all updated, only one bathroom, no family room -- certainly not roomy enough for almost 25 people!! He knew all of that and still wanted them to come, so we said, "Sure!" They came and had a wonderful time together -- lots of laughter, sharing, togetherness, and a wonderful break from school. They slept all over the house, ate all of our food, seemed to enjoy the whole weekend, and were appreciative of our hospitality. Seeing them walk to our church on Sunday morning as a group was a beautiful sight. Spending the weekend with such a great group of young people gave us hope in the next generation. How we all survived with only one bathroom is still a mystery!!

Our older daughter, Laura, also brought a group of at least 15 friends to our home for a weekend when she was a college student. They lined up their sleeping bags in the living room and other rooms and had a great time. (Girls and guys in separate rooms!) They all went to Great Adventure Amusement Park.

For a period of time, this house could have been called 'College Inn.' But the main point of this story is that you do not have to have a large, fancy, just-so house in order to entertain. What makes for a good time is lots of laughter, and meaningful sharing. That is called fellowship, and people are more interested and blessed by warm fellowship than by entertainment! You just need to open your home and share what you have with others. The blessing comes back double-fold to you as well. Remember, what you have is the Lord's anyway, so you are just sharing what the Lord has given to you. And what He has given to you is a heart to share Him and His love with others. That will last for eternity. Your house will not!"

Your children's friends have a powerful influence on them especially as they get older. There even comes a time when their peers' attitudes and influence trump yours.

> "Any of you who welcomes a little child like this because you are mine, is welcoming Me and caring for Me."
> Matthew 18:5 NIV

Types of Events

Easter Parties

When The Story of Jesus for Children first came out, I challenged two of my friends with little children to have a home party. One friend from church got her two young boys together and encouraged them to invite the neighbor kids. (She was especially organized and had box drinks and baggies of popcorn for each child to eat as they watched the film).

I challenged a young 9 year-old-friend to have an Easter party using the Jesus Film. She was concerned for the children at her bus stop and in her neighborhood who did not know the Lord. Madeleine caught my vision for evangelism. She and I went to my husband's office where we copied the template for the invitation. We phoned her mom to confirm the date and time. Then Madeleine carefully printed the pertinent information for her party on the master invitation and photocopied them.

The next day she and her mom went door to door and to the bus stop with the invitations. The day of the party I came to her house early and helped her put out Easter cookies and drinks. Madeleine got the idea to have an Easter egg hunt after the movie. That had a twofold benefit. The kids sat still through the movie (paying attention) because they knew the "hunt" was next. The moms arrived to find their children running around outside having a great time. Everyone left on a high note. Several children prayed along with the DVD on the TV. One little boy started going to AWANAS with Madeleine's family. Now his whole family goes to church.

Madeleine's girlfriend's mother would not let her attend the Easter party that year but later something exciting took place. While Madeleine was playing with her, they talked about spiritual things. Up in her tree house

Madeleine led that friend to Christ and the little girl prayed with her. The Easter party and the Jesus Film for Children were the catalyst. Through it, Madeleine learned how to lead someone in prayer to a personal relationship with Jesus even though she was only nine years old.

When children enter middle school or junior high school, their peers become a powerful force in their lives. Add to that the fact that their bodies are changing and hormones are affecting their emotions. This is a very strategic time in their lives; quite possibly the last time they will ever be so open to the Gospel. Madeleine was more apprehensive about having a "What God Wants for Christmas" Party. She was not as excited as she had been at the age of nine because she was worried about what the other kids would think.

Julie, Madeleine's mother, realized the eternal ramifications and helped Madeleine make sure the event was successful. She encouraged Madeleine because she realized it was for Madeleine's spiritual growth as well as for sharing Christ. At the end of the successful party, she was able to say to her daughter, "Look at what you did for those girls and how you grew through it." Julie and Madeleine's story of their Christmas party follows.

Jelly Bean Gift Bag

Make up a "take-home gift bag" of jelly beans using the colors on the following page. Include the explanation on a card attached to the bag.

Jelly Beans

Black Beans

for the bad things we do (sins) that darken our hearts and make us live in darkness. Acts 26:17-18 "I am sending you to them to open their eyes and turn them from darkness to light." Romans 3:23 NIV "For all have sinned and fall short of the glory of God."

Purple Beans

for the purple (a royal color) robe the soldiers put on Jesus when they made fun of Him. Mark 15:17 NIV "They put a purple robe on Him then they twisted a crown of thorns and set it on him."

Red Beans

for the blood Jesus shed on the cross for our sins. The crown and the nails in his hands and feet made Him bleed. I John 1:7 NIV "... the blood of Jesus, God's Son, purifies us from all unrighteousness."

White Beans

for the way he makes our hearts clean and white when we ask Him in to forgive us for the bad things we do. Isaiah 1:18 NIV "Though your sins are like scarlet red, they will be as white as snow."

Yellow Beans

for the golden streets of heaven where we will go when we die, if we have asked Jesus into our lives.

Green Beans

for growing as a Christian believer when we read the Bible and pray. Psalm 23:2 NIV "He makes me lie down in green pastures." Acts 17:11 NIV "They searched the Bible everyday."

Orange Beans

like the color of fire for the power we get from the Holy Spirit to live good lives. Acts 1:8 NIV "You will receive power when the Holy Spirit comes to you."

Pink Beans

for the joyful life Jesus gives to all who believe. John 15:11 NIV Jesus' "joy will remain in you."

Christmas Parties

A couple of years later Madeleine's mother had a Christmas party with 6th grade girls. Here's what she wrote about that party.

Having a 6th grade girl has changed my life. She requires things of me I never imagined and yet I'm enjoying her more than I ever have. We laugh together, cry together, love and hope together AND we evangelize together. As I strive toward being a godly woman myself, I am more and more aware of the fact that she's watching, learning and growing right along side me.

Part of growing into the body of a godly woman is becoming aware of the spiritual needs around you... even if you're only in junior high! From an early age, my daughter demonstrated a heart for sharing her love of God. More recent scenarios have caused her to show signs of intimidation because "God" is not too cool in the public schools these days. So, our task was to come up with a way to draw her overly-cool classmates into our home, keep them interested and then gently present the truth of God's Word to their impressionable yet secular hearts.

We planned our event around the excitement of the coming "winter" vacation, capitalizing on the fact that, although everyone was busy, they'd all be in the mood for a party. We phoned 12 girls in her class and invited them to meet us after school at "kiss-n-ride" on the last day before vacation. Most didn't even ask what we were going to do; they were just excited to be invited to a party.

Once we were home, I gathered the girls around me and said something like this:

"Isn't this fun? Are you all excited about Christmas? Well, our goal today is to spend some time decorating Christmas cookies, then I want to talk a little bit about Christmas and what it really means, then we get to watch a video called "The Nativity Story"···This is the true story, (straight from the Bible), about what Mary, the mother of Jesus really went through during the months surrounding the birth of Jesus."

Spread around the kitchen were small containers of colored icing. We had pre-baked cookies in the shapes of nativity characters so we were ready to "dig in" to our activity. The girls seemed to really enjoy the creative, yet "themed" event. This time also provided a great opportunity for the adults to observe the conversations and interactions of such an interesting and complex age-group.

Once the finished cookies were stored in their take-home containers, we all sat down for a little talk. After an ice-breaker, a girlfriend of mine artfully discussed the real meaning of Christmas. What an amazing opportunity to share Christ with such a captive audience! I sat watching these young ladies take in the gospel and longed for them to hear its true message. Although my daughter was visibly tentative, anticipating her girlfriend's potential reactions, I felt it was a great environment to not only train her to be bold and assertive, but also to share Christ in a real and personal way.

We finished our afternoon by watching "The Nativity Story". The girls continuously asked to pause the film so they could ask some interesting and important questions. Again, another perfect opportunity to share Christ; I was able to point out Mary's faith in God, Joseph's integrity, the hurtful behavior of the townspeople in Nazareth, the sovereignty of God's plan and the inconvenient delivery of a child that took divine strength and perseverance. The girls soaked up my anecdotes and basked in the splendor of the virgin birth.

One by one the parents came to pick the girls up. I had not spoken with any of the parents at this point so I wanted to take the opportunity to build rapport, open the potential for dialogue and give a brief summary of what had taken place. In most cases, I welcomed each parent with something like this:

> "Hi, thanks for coming to get your daughter. We had such a great time! We decorated nativity cookies, we chatted about how Christmas has been lost in the hustle and bustle of society and we encouraged the girls to remember the true meaning of Christmas. Then we watched "The Nativity Story". Have you seen it? It's a great, down-to-earth message about Mary and the circumstances surrounding Christ's birth. All in all, I think the girls had a great time".

Each parent seemed thrilled with the event, thankful for the "time off" and some even hung around to visit. In fact, one woman wanted to talk about the "virgin birth" and some of its implications.

The girls left with a smile on their face and a "party favor" containing a pair of Christmas earrings, some candy and a gospel tract booklet entitled "Would You Like to Know God Personally?" I went to bed that evening thankful for such a purposeful afternoon. People's lives were touched, (mine included) and the great commission was fulfilled. Praise God!

Children are the easiest age group to reach for Christ! Remember, you serve them with love and attention. Be sure to answer all their questions. It shows you really care about them and they will love anything you do with them. All they require is to be welcomed and loved. Anything you do is appreciated and the simplest little things are welcomed, enjoyed, and remembered for a long time. Kids do not come with the same walls that their parents have to the Gospel, so you can be bolder and more Christ-like. If their parents decide to stay at your event, keep the content the same. Let them observe in the background. Who knows how God will touch their hearts while they are watching!

Valentine Parties

We all remember with fond memories the Valentines we made and received in our childhood days. What better time is there to teach children about the unconditional love of Jesus! Show The Story of Jesus for Children movie to let the children know who the giver of love is. Serve heart shaped cookies or a heart shaped cake that says, "Jesus Loves You" on it. Let the children make Valentine name tags or a Valentine for their parents as you wait for everyone to arrive. Introduce the film with a child-style personal story of how you've come to know what real love is all about and who it comes from. If you've got some time on your hands and feel creative, make a large cookie for each child to take home that says, "Jesus Loves _____" with his or her own name on it. Do not forget to order some of the booklets entitled, "The Greatest Story" from the Jesus Film web site to go in their take-home cookie bag.

Help their Parents

If you want to make friends with the parents of the families you are hoping to minister to, try this: have a Valentine's Slumber Party so that their parents can go out on a Valentine's Date night. If you're not up for the whole evening then have an extended late party so the parents can go out to dinner. Remember, restaurants are more expensive on the actual holiday night, so try a day or so earlier.

For more info: www. jesusforchildren.org

Princess Parties

These work at any age and are adaptable to what the different age groups are interested in. Little girls love the Disney princesses and love playing "dress up". Get some old prom dresses out of your attic, at yard sales, or thrift stores. Make tiaras and put on face and body glitter and tell them the story of Queen Esther. Consider using the "Princess" talk on the website if they are old enough. Older girls love makeovers and makeup parties. Talk to them while they are painting their nails and waiting for them to dry. (Remember Queen Esther had a special makeover before she became the queen.)

Princess Parties work well when discipling a group of young girls. One friend was a volunteer helper with her church junior high group. She invited the girls over to her apartment one night for a Princess Party. Relationships deepened and the youth group was transformed. Another woman invited her daughter's high school friends to her home. After facials and discussion about fashion and appearance, she gave a princess talk. That night six teens gave their lives to Christ. No matter what age, all girls love the idea of being a princess.

For More Ideas

Go on the web and find lots of ideas for children's parties on sites like www.kidsdomain.com/holidays and www.cefonline.com. Do not forget to check this book's companion web site at www.EntertainingForEternity.com to see what other mothers have tried.

You're Invited
to a
Princess Party!

Date:
Time:

What to wear:

Where:

Please RSVP to:

Halloween Parties

While this is far from a Christian occasion, we can make the most of Halloween to effect our world for Christ. Everyone loves to dress up and eat free candy. How can we deny that?! However, there is a dark side of this holiday and we want to stay as far away from that as possible. Satan is very real and this is one of his high holidays, so we need to redeem it with a positive experience that will turn the children's minds to those positive spiritual influences. Precious minds are so vulnerable and we do not want to cause nightmares so avoid letting your child wear "scary" costumes or watch horror movie.

A girl, recently having accepted Jesus into her life, was asked by a friend what it was like to "believe". She replied, "It's like being a pumpkin: God picks you from the patch, brings you in, and washes all the dirt off you. Then He cuts the top off and scoops out all the yucky stuff. He removes the seeds of doubt, hate, greed, etc. Then...He carves you a new smiling face and puts His light inside of you to shine for all the world to see.

Halloween Ideas to Try

· Celebrate All Saints Day which is on November 1st. Children dress up as Bible characters when they go out to gather candy or go to parties.
· One year, we had our own costume party in our basement. I read the Bible story about the Witch of Endor (I Samuel 28) to the kids and we discussed the occult and its dangers. When age appropriate, children need to be educated and warned in this.
· Check your local Christian store for good children's books or brochures at this time of year. Hand out clever children's brochures along with your candy.
· Think of creative uses for the pumpkin verses. Print it on a card with pumpkin graphics from your computer or put a pumpkin sticker on the card with it. This could be the beginnings of a stirring evangelistic talk and a take home piece for afterwards.

Celebrate Jesus Home Parties

It's the easiest entertaining you'll ever do. Use the JESUS Film Project's <u>The Story of Jesus for Children</u> movie. All you have to do is pop some popcorn and invite the neighborhood children in. If you have children involved in sports, scouts, or other organizations, invite those children in, too. The children on the video do all the evangelism for you. It's one of the clearest Gospel presentations you will ever find.

Go to: www.jesusforchildren.org Click on "products.
Or call 1-800-432-1997

Some of the materials available are:
DVDs of <u>The Story of Jesus for Children</u>
    Available in almost any language
<u>Celebrate Jesus Home Parties for Children</u> manual
    I wrote it to guide you through everything you need
    to know to throw a Celebrate Jesus Party
"The Greatest Promise" booklet
    A follow-up booklet to send home with each child
"Promise" Commitment Cards
    For the children to fill out at the party

What is a Celebrate Jesus Party?

This is an informal gathering of children to view the The Story of Jesus for Children video. The purpose is to lead them to a saving knowledge of Jesus Christ. The party can be held at Christmas, Easter or any other time of year.

This is an opportunity to gather the un-churched children, in an informal, non-threatening arena. "Latch-key" children are eager to come into a traditional home and have some fun with their peers. What's more fun than popcorn and a movie? Play a couple of games until everyone arrives, end with some special treats and prizes and you've got a sure success with the children and the gospel.

Here's a chance for moms, dads, singles and young adults to have a dynamic ministry that will count for all eternity. These are the people who drive the carpools, coach the teams, lead scout troops, and those who know all the children in their neighborhoods.

Armed with a few simple tools and The Story of Jesus for Children movie, they have the opportunity to see young lives changed. It may have impact on the future of our nation, and even the world, for Jesus.

Follow-up Information

Make sure to connect help children who are interested or need follow up. They can go to www.wonderzone.com or to:

Child Evangelism Fellowship Mailbox Club
Call CEF at 636-4456-4321.
Ask for the "Mailbox Club."
Website: www.CEFonline.com
(Go to materials, free downloads or free training)

Order free Bibles for any child who wants to take one home by writing to:
Bibles for Children, Inc.
1054 State Hwy 41
Afton, NY 13730
or calling: 607-639-2726

Using the Jesus Film for Children

By now it is apparent that I believe in using <u>The Story of Jesus for Children</u> at home parties. This comes naturally, since I came to Christ at age nine because of a moving film at a Good News Club. Let me share the story of how my granddaughter, Lily gave her life to Jesus at the age of four.

My daughter, Kristi, my husband, Lily and I were on a long seven hour drive in the car and I had run out of DVD's to keep Lily happy. The only other DVD I had was a copy of <u>The Story of Jesus for Children</u>. Because of Lily's young age, I wondered if it would be too complex or emotionally charged. Another mom had mentioned that the crucifixion scene was too intense for children and that she could not use it for little children.

I decided to turn it over to the Lord, and I put the DVD in the player. Little Lily sat quietly with her head phones on as the car continued down the interstate. I kept an eye out for when she would get to the part about Passion Week. Kristi interjected at one point that those were "mean men who didn't love Jesus". I watched Lily's concerned face but she seemed to be handling things very well. There was a worried look in her eyes as Jesus died on the cross. At the end of the movie, children narrating the movie explained that you need to pray and ask Jesus into your life. Lily sat still and very attentive through it all even though she was only four and a half years old. Then a thrilling thing happened. As the sinner's prayer was given, she said it out loud along with the children on the small screen. How thrilling to be able to witness my own granddaughter invite Jesus Christ into her life!

Later that night when we arrived at her house, we asked Lily to tell her other grand-parents what had happened that day. She didn't need any prompting. She knew what she had done and boldly told them. They, too, were thrilled. In the ensuing conversation my husband Sam said something like, "Isn't it wonderful that Lily asked Jesus into her heart?" Lily turned from her play and quickly corrected him saying, "No, Papa, I didn't ask Jesus into my heart. I asked Him into my LIFE!" She really knew and understood what she had done.

To this day I still get choked up telling this precious story. Do not underestimate what little children can understand nor worry about sharing the Gospel with them.

Chapter 12
Making Sure of Heaven

The following section will equip you with the tools needed to help someone make sure that they will go to heaven when they die. These are basic tools to help anyone share their faith without offending.

These will include:

- Dealing with your fears
- Conversation Stimulators to use at your events
- Sharing your personal story of coming to faith in Christ
- Sharing the Gospel one-on-one
- Speaking preparation for your speaker-driven events
- Motivating your small group with the biblical basis for Entertaining for Eternity
- Following up your event and the decisions made at it

Why should we share our faith?

Let me ask you a couple of rhetorical questions.

1. What's the greatest thing that's ever happened to you? (I guess we would all say coming to know Christ in a real, personal, and life-changing way.)

2. What's the greatest thing that you could do for another person? (If I am so pleased by my decision, the greatest gift I could give to those I care about is that same personal relationship with the living, loving Savior.)

3. Why did Jesus come? Luke 19:10 says, "The Son of Man came to seek and to save that which is lost." Why are we keeping the cure to the cancer of the human soul a secret? We gladly have Basket, Candle, and Kitchen Products parties. Why not share your home to see lives changed for all eternity?

The following text appears in the image:

personally or experience
His love and plan,

People are Sinful
"...for all have sinned and fall short of the
glory of God" (Romans 3:23)

People were created to have fellowship with God
but, because of our stubborn self-will, we chose
to go our own independent way and fellowship
with God was broken. This self-will, characterized
by an attitude of active rebellion or passive indif-
ference, is evidence of what the Bible calls sin.

People are Separated
"...the wages of sin is death" (spiritual sepa-
...on from God) (Romans 6:23)

God

People

This diagram illu...
that God is holy a...
are sinful. A great...
arates the two. The...
illustrate that people...
continually trying to r...
God and establish a pe...
sonal relationship with...
through our own effort...
such as a good li...
phy, or...

Why Did Jesus Come?

Let's think about Jesus' priorities. The main reason that he came to earth and went through the agony of the cross was to reconcile people to God. He came to bring forgiveness and new life to anyone who would receive Him into their life and put Him first place in their life.

If you knew that you were about to die and would have an opportunity to say one last thing to your loved ones, you would give it much thought and want to summarize what was most important in your life. We, however, have Jesus' last words for each of us. They are found in what is called the Great Commission from Matthew 28:18-20:

> "All authority in heaven and on earth has been given to me. Therefore go and make disciples of all nations, baptizing them in the name of the Father and of the Son and of the Holy Spirit, and teaching them to obey everything I have commanded you. And surely I am with you always to the very end of the age" (NIV).

He also promised in Acts 1:8 to empower us for the job by sending the Holy Spirit to live within us. In Matthew 10:19-20 Jesus told us, "Do not worry about what to say or how to say it. At that time you will be given what to say, for it will not be you speaking, but the Spirit of your Father speaking through you." I Peter 3:15 says, "Always be prepared to give an answer to everyone who asks you to give the reason for the hope that you have. But do this with gentleness and respect" (NIV).

As you begin to open up your home you will see Him give you the right words to say. Some of the material in this manual will enable you to "be prepared to give an answer... for the hope that is within you." The goal of Entertaining for Eternity is to equip and encourage you. We need not be ashamed of the Gospel of Jesus Christ, it has the power to change lives. (See Romans 1:16). In Colossians 4:6 we are told, "Let your conversation be always full of grace, and seasoned with salt, so that you may know how to answer everyone" (NIV). The following sections will encourage you to take some steps of faith and begin to be "salt and light" to those around you.

Salt Makes People Thirsty

Think about what salt does. It adds flavor and makes you thirsty. That's what heavenly hospitality should do for people you invite into your home. Make that the goal of your event. A "seeker" should leave your home thinking, "Wow! That was interesting. How can I have what they have?" What transpired at your event should have been "tasty" spiritually. They should begin to become "thirsty" for Jesus. Some events will be geared to ask for some sort of decision regarding Christ, and others may only be tantalizing them -- preparing their hearts and making them "thirsty". We call these types of events "pre-evangelistic" (like the patriotic picnics or some dinner parties mentioned in earlier chapters.)

Our Culture Today

Studies show that people have a superficial knowledge of the Bible. People need to hear the Gospel several times before they are ready to respond. Bill Faye, the author of Share Jesus Without Fear, says a person needs to hear the Gospel an average of 7.6 times before he is ready to respond. At our events we are merely "fruit checking". That means we are looking to see which fruit is ripe. Remember that Jesus said He would make us fishers of men. He didn't say "hunters" of men. What's the difference? Fishermen throw out lines and only bring in those fish that are hungry and bite. A hunter stalks through the woods looking for anything to shoot. A fisherman patiently waits and watches the little bobber on his line to see when it's ready to start reeling in. That's what we are doing at our events.

In this final chapter, "Making Sure of Heaven", you will find hints for personal or individual evangelism. You will be using a little booklet called "Would You Like to Know God Personally?" This is printed by New Life Resources which is a ministry of Campus Crusade for Christ. (It is a version of the Four Spiritual Laws written by Bill Bright.) Also you will find worksheets to help you write out "Your Story". You need to do this so that your story will come naturally in your conversations at events. This is something that all believers should do to help them in their encounters with seekers. All this is in response to the verse in I Peter 3:15 where we are admonished to "always be prepared to give an answer for the reason for the hope that you have with gentleness and respect" (NIV).

It is important to remember the definition of successful witnessing. Successful witnessing is sharing Christ in the power of the Holy Spirit and leaving the results to God. When we realize this, the burden is off our shoulders and resting where it belongs - squarely on God's shoulders! This allows us to relax and share our faith naturally as an overflow of the abundant life that we enjoy with Christ. With this mindset, our friends and acquaintances will not feel like we are manipulating or expecting an immediate response from them.

Successful Witnessing is sharing Christ in the power of the Holy Spirit and leaving the results to God.

Tools to Help You Share Your Faith

- Conversation Stimulators - Turning Conversations to spiritual things
- Sharing Your Personal Story - How to Write Your 3-minute story
- Sharing One on One - Using the "Would You Like to Know God Personally" booklet
- Speaker Events - How to Develop and Give a Talk
- Motivating Your Small Group/Biblical Basis
- Follow Up

Conversation Stimulators

Let me explain conversation stimulators. They have two purposes: to probe and to provoke thought. These are simple and do not have a right or wrong answer. They are merely ways to probe the thoughts of seekers and find out where they are spiritually. They are used to uncover areas of the Gospel they do not understand. You cannot scratch a person unless you know where they itch. These questions are used to find out where they "itch" spiritually.

When using the conversation stimulator questions, you and the other believers are mainly listening. Use what Bill Faye calls the "Hmmm Principle". Ask the question and wait to hear the seeker's response. Don't be afraid of silence. It seems longer than it really is. If nothing happens, try another question from a different angle. Don't give a clue where you stand on the answer even if they are completely incorrect. Simply say, "Hmm." Many people do not figure out what they really believe until they have to articulate it to someone else. In doing so, they begin to question for themselves what they believe. People love to give their opinions and feel honored that you want to know about them.

The Holy Spirit also begins to work while all this is going on. This is another good reason why you need to pray before your event takes place. Soon your guests will come to a point where they want to know what you believe and will begin to ask questions. Sometimes though, this doesn't happen until after the event is over (perhaps the next time you are with them, they respond.) Then they may bring up spiritual topics and you can discuss them further. If there are many people at your event, it may be better to have one-on-one time later. You can then take them through a simple Gospel presentation like the "How to Know God Personally" booklet printed by Campus Crusade for Christ.

Conversation stimulators work well when used after dinner and through dessert. If your event is not dinner but merely a Dessert, then use these after everyone has been served dessert.

Let a man ask the first question. It will dispel the feeling that only women are interested in "spiritual matters." If there is time, take turns with subsequent questions. Don't make it look like an interrogation. You can memorize several conversation stimulators ahead of time so that you can share them informally. Weave them into the natural conversation of the evening or take some of these questions and write them out on slips of paper. Fold them and put them in a bowl or basket and have each guest choose one.

Conversation Stimulators are useful for determining where your friend is on his or her spiritual journey. They can be used to take their "spiritual temperature" and help you in sharing the Gospel with people. When guiding a conversation with a friend to spiritual things, it is important to not turn them off. The attitude we should have is one of honest Christ-like inquiry into their ideas. We want to genuinely learn about them, how they think and what is important to them. We are looking for ways to have them understand that we are truly interested in what they are thinking and feeling. We should not try to convince them of anything or to judge their opinions. That's the Holy Spirit's job. We are to communicate that we are honored that they would share their thoughts with us.

Because each of us has a unique personality, you may find some of the following conversation starters more to your liking. Use a highlighter and mark the ones you feel most comfortable using. Begin committing them to memory so that you will be ready when an opportunity presents itself. The next time you are out for coffee with a friend or walking together in the neighborhood, you will have something to stimulate the conversation towards the spiritual things of life.

One friend suggested this idea:

Choose several of your favorite questions and write them on separate slips of paper. Roll these up in your croissant rolls so that the tip of the slip of paper is showing. As you pass your bread basket everyone will be surprised with a question. The conversation will automatically flow because there will be a sense of spontaneity and surprise much like "fortune cookies," that we enjoy after a Chinese dinner.

Be sure to check out this book's companion website for more Conversation Stimulators and find out how others' events went. Tell us about yours! www.Entertaining ForEternity.com

Simple Conversation Stimulators

1. Where are you in your spiritual pilgrimage?
2. In a conversation with someone who has never heard about God, what would you say about Him from your own experience?
3. If and when you get to heaven, what are the first couple of questions you want to ask God?
4. Has anything ever happened to you that was dramatic, personal or spectacular that caused you to be certain that there is a God who is both infinite and personally caring?
5. If you could know God personally, would you be interested?
6. In your opinion, who is Jesus Christ?
7. Would you consider yourself a fully devoted follower of Jesus Christ?
8. What do you find most attractive about Christianity or the person of Christ? What do you find least attractive?
9. What do you think about the institution of the church? Have you ever attended one? Was it a positive or negative experience?
10. What do you consider to be two major turning points in your life?
11. If you were to die today, do you know for sure that you would go to heaven?
12. How do you know that you will go to heaven when you die?
13. Why should God let you into heaven?
14. Have you ever made an "adult" decision of faith about Jesus Christ? (This is a good question for those who were raised in a church.)

Quaker Questions

Many people use "Quaker Questions" as an icebreaker for parties. It is a creative way to dig deeper and get to know more about people's backgrounds. The questions seem to get a little harder to answer as you go!

The Quaker Questions are:
1) Where did you live when you were six years old and who lived with you?
2) How was your home heated? What were the winters like?
3) What person, place, or thing was the center of warmth in your life when you were a child?
4) When did God become a "warm" being to you and how did this happen?

These questions could be asked by the host or typed up and all four given to each guest allowing each to choose which one they would like to answer. That way nonbelievers are not made to feel uncomfortable and the believers have an opportunity to share their faith. Who knows? Maybe a nonbeliever may open up. This is an excellent way to get to know your friends on a deeper level. It's exciting to see what God will do.

Additional Conversation Stimulators

1. What are two or three major truths upon which you have based your decision-making?
2. Who is the most impressive person you have ever known?
3. What single thing would you like to make absolutely certain you do during your lifetime?
4. What historical character, from any period of history, can you imagine yourself to be?
5. What are you reading that is not an assignment? What have you read that caused you to grow as a person?
6. How are you growing personally?
7. What is your greatest strength? What are you doing to develop it?
8. What is something you consider to be a great personal success? Why is it so significant?
9. How would you describe your father and his impact on your life?
10. How would you describe your mother and her impact on your life?
11. Tell me about two of your lifelong friends and why they have had such an impact on your life. What made you choose them as friends?
12. Do you have a mentor? Tell me about this person's impact on your life.
13. What do you think would probably surprise most people about you? Why?
14. How do you handle pressure?
15. What do you need from your friends?
16. How do you maintain balance in your life?
17. Have you dealt with the questions: How much money is enough? What do I do with the money that's left after that? How would you define materialism? How do you deal with it in your life?
18. If you were to inherit a million dollars today, and could not spend it in your own enterprise, what would you do with it and why?
19. What have you found to be the best way to absorb disappointment, rejection, distress and discouragement? How effective has that way been?

Seeker Question

"If you could ask God one question, what would it be?"

Try asking this question during dessert. It's fascinating what comes out. Many people are struggling with God over some difficulty in their lives. Maybe they just have an honest intellectual question that's been bugging them all their lives. Most questions fall into a few basic categories and are universal.

After everyone has shared their individual question, challenge the group to meet perhaps once a month to tackle one question at a time. What fun to watch seekers come to understand who God really is and how loving He is!

Hopefully they will be touched by how much you care about what bothers them and surprised that there truly are answers to life's tough questions. You will grow immensely as you research the answers. Go to books like:

Evidence that Demands a Verdict by Josh McDowell
The Case for Christ and The Case for Faith, both by Lee Stroebel
Letters From A Skeptic by Dr. Gregory Boyd
Know Why You Believe by Paul Little

You could also go to these web sites:

www.apologetics.com
www.leaderU.com

Telling Your Personal Faith Story in a Clear and Relevant Way

Why Your Story is Important

1. Our culture values experiences. Our friends are genuinely interested
2. They can relate to it. There is some common thread in all of our lives.
3. They may not believe the Bible but the unbeliever can't ignore the changes in your life. Your story can't be refuted because it is real to you.

Do's and Don'ts

Your Story should be told in a way that will make them want to know Christ for themselves. Get inside the unbelievers head and find out what he's looking for.

1. Pray and ask the Lord to give you wisdom and guidance as you write out your story
2. Be positive from start to finish.
3. Keep it clear and simple and easy to say.
4. Be brief and to the point. Try to keep it to three or four minutes.
5. Begin with an interesting, attention-getting sentence and have a good conclusion.
6. Keep it culturally relevant and up to date. Revise it from time to time as the years go by.
7. Keep in mind your "target audience" (those you will be sharing with). Try to think like they do.
8. For your theme, choose something characteristic of your experience that is of general interest to non-believers. What is it that they are struggling with or want out of life? Emphasize those aspects of your story that will relate to their concerns and interests. Some themes might be: peace, confidence, control, fear, patience, security, etc.
9. Be realistic. Remember that Christ does not eliminate all the problems of life, but He enables you to live through them with peace and confidence.
10. Do not mention denominations in a derogatory way. Do not make statements that reflect negatively on the church or other organizations.
11. Use ordinary, everyday language that un-churched people can understand. Do not use religious clichés or "God-talk."
    Do not use words like: saved, revival, born again, repent, etc. Instead, think of secular terms to explain what you mean.

The How of Your Story

The most important part of Your Story is the "How"! In sharing our faith, we rely on the Holy Spirit to "draw all men unto Christ" (John 12:32; 14:26, Romans 8:2; I Corinthians 3:16). However, we need to do our part in making it easy for the hearer to understand what they need to do in order to put their trust in the Lord Jesus Christ. Paul says that we need to "be prepared to give a ready answer for the hope that is within us, yet with gentleness and reverence." (I Peter 3:15)

Keep in mind that your goal is to give enough information so that the listener can walk away knowing exactly what they need to do to start a vital and living relationship with our Savior. That's all the Lord wants us to do. He will do the rest. Ask yourself, "From what I've said, would they know how to pray and ask Christ into their lives?" You might use sentences like these:

> "When I asked Christ into my life, I prayed a prayer like this: 'Lord Jesus, thank you for dying on the cross for all my wrong doings. I want to know you in a real and personal way to be sure of Eternal Life. Come into my heart and life and make me the kind of person that you want me to be.'"

Notice the basic content of this prayer:
1. There is a realization of sin and forgiveness.
2. There is recognition of what Jesus did on the cross.
3. There is an invitation into the life and surrender to Christ.

These three concepts need to be expressed but can be worded in various ways. Salvation comes to a person when he or she realizes these truths and verbalizes them to God.

> "If you confess with your mouth Jesus as Lord, and believe in your heart that God raised Him from the dead, you shall be saved; for with the heart man believes, resulting in righteousness, and with the mouth he confesses, resulting in salvation." Romans 10:9-10

A Childhood Conversion

If you gave your life to Christ as a child and do not know how to make Your Story sound relevant to a secular person, do any of the following:

- Speak in general terms in the "Before Christ" section without giving the specific age that you were when you made the commitment.
- Talk about the time later in life when you dedicated your life to becoming a fully devoted follower of Christ.
- Focus more on the "After Christ" section.

More Questions to Ask Yourself

Before you start writing, picture a person you know who is at the same situation in life as you are. What is his or her name? What is he or she struggling with? How is Christ making a difference in this same area for you? Still having trouble? Think about some areas like job, relationships, marriage or dealing with children. What resources do you, as a believer, have that the secular person does not have in handling problems in these areas?

Telling Your Story Worksheet

Theme:

Attention Getting Device:

Before:

1. Where were you spiritually before receiving Christ, and how did that affect you, your feelings, attitudes, actions, and relationships?

2. What caused you to begin considering God/Christ as a solution to your needs?

How:

3. What realization did you come to that finally motivated you to receive Christ?

4. Specifically, how did you receive Christ?

After:

5. How did your life begin to change after you trusted Christ?

6. What other benefits have you experienced since becoming a Christian? (Particularly think of those benefits that would best relate to people in your target audience.)

Verse:

Theme Wrap Up / Conclusion:

Still having trouble getting started? Go to the website and read three examples totally different types of personal stories.

Speaker Preparation

The speaker needs to consider the holidays or popular topics that will interest unbelievers. Feel free to suggest or use some of the talks in this book as well as those on the web site. The talk should be relevant and lead to a clear Gospel presentation with an opportunity to make a decision for Christ. If your event is for both men and women, it works best to have a man be your main speaker.

For more informal presentations have a couple of believers share their story of coming to faith in Christ. After they have shared their stories, allow time for discussion and challenge the unbelievers to consider what knowing Christ in a real and personal manner could do for them. When using these story type testimonials, have an equal number of men and women sharing. Their stories should not be longer than 3 minutes.

The Elements of a Good Evangelistic Talk

- Attention Getting Device (AGD) -- An opening statement or premise that will draw the listener in to listen to your talk.
- Body of your talk -- based on a holiday, season or interesting topic that seekers are curious about.
- Clear Gospel -- Who Jesus is and what He did for us. Why we need Him and how he can impact our lives.
- Opportunity for the audience to respond -- prayer of commitment to Christ.
- Close -- wrap up the topic and answer the AGD or premise you started with.
- Audience Evaluation and Response -- Comment cards and Follow Up.

The Basic Elements of the Gospel

1. God loves you.
2. Sin separates us from his love.
3. Jesus Christ's provisions
4. What we need to do to experience forgiveness of sins and a have personal relationship with God.

Comment Cards

These are little 3x5 cards that you pass out along with a pen or pencil at the end of the talk. Either you or your speaker can handle this part. Decide ahead of time on this. Sometimes I decorate the cards with holiday stickers or stamps to make them look inviting and important. You will want to tell them to put their name and a short note on their card telling you what they thought of the event and the talk. Ask for their phone numbers for future parties; that is if you don't have them. For large events you may want to print a card ahead of time providing lines and optional boxes. (See sample.)

Everybody loves to give their opinions and you will want to know what your friends thought about the event and the talk. Comment cards are a crucial part of your event. It's very important that they are handled properly. This is a venue for your friends to tell you if they are interested in more socials or helping you with future events.

In our private society people don't want to raise their hands or come forward to register their decision for Christ. Yet as a hostess, you need to know if any of your guests prayed along silently with your speaker. In Romans 10:9-10 we see the importance of telling someone of a decision for Christ. "If you confess with your mouth that Jesus is Lord and believe in your heart that God raised him from the dead, you will be saved. For it is by believing in your heart that you are made right with God, and it is by confessing with your mouth that you are saved." (NLB)
Besides asking everyone for their comments about the event you need to ask them to put an "X" beside their name if they prayed along silently with the speaker. You may also have them indicate if they would like to be in a beginner's Bible Study, if you are offering one. These pieces of information are very important for you to have as you consider following up your event.

Don't get scared and rush through the comment card portion of your program. Be very clear about the point about marking an "X" if they prayed. Go over it two times. Then give them plenty of time to write out their comments. Have everybody writing, even your Christian friends who attend. Play some soft music in the background. After you are sure that everyone understands and is starting to write, give them clear directions about where you want them to put their cards. This can be a basket on the coffee table or near the door as they leave.

Read through your comment cards alone or with your speaker ONLY after everybody has left. You will be greatly encouraged by what the Lord has done in the lives of those in attendance. Comment cards enable you to find out if there were any decisions made for Christ at your event.

Comment Card

Name: email: phone:

- ☐ I prayed along silently with the speaker to know Christ personally.
- ☐ I already know Christ personally.
- ☐ I would like more information about knowing Christ personally.
- ☐ I would like to help with future socials.
- ☐ I would be interested in a beginner's 4-6 week Bible Study.

My comments about the event and talk:

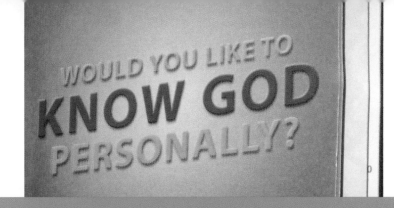

The booklet "Would You Like to Know God Personally" is useful in many situations. It can be read to a friend one on one over coffee or shared with a small group of people. It is also an excellent tool to use when following up someone who has indicated on their comment card that they prayed with a speaker. It can also be handed out as a take home piece after an event. It's best to read it over ahead of time and become very familiar with it so that you can share and read it at ease. That way you can adequately focus on the person you are sharing it with.

How to Use the Booklet
"Would you like to know God personally?"

Pages 1 & 2:
Introducing the Booklet

As you pull a booklet from your pocket or purse, you may wish to use one of these statements that have proven effective in bridging the conversation:

1. "You know, I came across a booklet that clearly explains how we can have a personal relationship with God. It's called Would You Like to Know God Personally?"

2. If you think the person may be a Christian but you're not sure, you could say, "I've just recently found a way to express my faith that really makes sense, and I'd like to share it with you."

There are times, such as on a noisy airplane, when I simply hand the booklet to a person and ask him to read it and tell me what he thinks. After he has read it, I'll touch on the highlights, then read pages 8-10 word for word.

Page 3:
A Positive Starting Point

Page 3 establishes that God loves the listener and offers a wonderful plan for his life. Continually pray for God's love to be expressed through you. Take a pen or pencil, hold the booklet so the listener can follow along with you, and begin reading aloud. You're sharing with, not preaching to or even reading to the listener. You are introducing the person to the Lord Jesus Christ, and the booklet is simply a communication tool.

When questions arise that would change the subject, explain that in most cases the questions will be answered as you continue. If you're not sure whether the question is answered in the booklet, you can say, "That's an excellent question. Let's talk about it after we've read through the booklet."

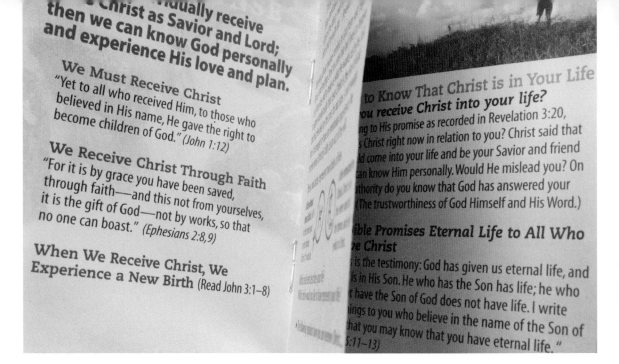

We Must Receive Christ
"Yet to all who received Him, to those who believed in His name, He gave the right to become children of God." *(John 1:12)*

We Receive Christ Through Faith
"For it is by grace you have been saved, through faith—and this not from yourselves, it is the gift of God—not by works, so that no one can boast." *(Ephesians 2:8,9)*

When We Receive Christ, We Experience a New Birth *(Read John 3:1–8)*

...tually receive ...Christ as Savior and Lord; then we can know God personally and experience His love and plan.

to Know That Christ is in Your Life
...ou receive Christ into your life?
...ng to His promise as recorded in Revelation 3:20, ...Christ right now in relation to you? Christ said that ...d come into your life and be your Savior and friend ...can know Him personally. Would He mislead you? On ...thority do you know that God has answered your ...(The trustworthiness of God Himself and His Word.)

...ble Promises Eternal Life to All Who ...e Christ
...is the testimony: God has given us eternal life, and ...is in His Son. He who has the Son has life; he who ...t have the Son of God does not have life. I write ...ings to you who believe in the name of the Son of ...hat you may know that you have eternal life. "
...5:11–13)

Pages 4 & 5:

Why Man is Seperated from God

Continue reading. Glance at your listener occasionally as you read, both to help personalize what you're sharing and to gauge whether he's following along. If there seems to be no response, stop and ask, "Is this making sense?" If the listener is interested but has time constraints, give him the booklet and encourage him to read through it that night. If he's not interested at all, give him the booklet and say, "Perhaps there'll come a time when spiritual things are of special interest to you. Why don't you keep this?"

Pages 4 and 5 emphasize the reason why people may not experience God's love and plan – sin. Romans 3:23 shows that sin is universal: All have sinned and fall short of God's ideal. Romans 6:23 shows that the consequence of sin is death, or eternal separation from God. This is the toughest part for the listener to hear, but it is essential that he understand his separation from God.

You'll find the diagrams especially helpful in explaining the gospel. They give the listener a visual "hook" to grasp the truths of God's Word.

Pages 6 & 7:

The Most Joyful News Ever Announced

Here it is! God's provision for man's sin. How, through Jesus Christ, man can circumvent the kingdom of darkness and enter the kingdom of light. Pages 6 and 7 illustrate how Christ died for man's sin, rose from the dead, and is the only way to fellowship with God. He has bridged the gulf of separation through His Son, Jesus.

Pages 8 & 9:

Personalizing the Good News

These pages emphasize the fact that it is not enough to merely give intellectual assent to the first three principles. One must personally receive Jesus Christ as Savior and Lord to know and live out God's love and plan. The listener is shown how to receive Christ, and what it involves.

Pay special attention to the two circles at the bottom of page 9. These are especially effective in helping the listener acknowledge where he stands with God. You'll find that it comes in handy in a variety of situations. Some people have even used the diagram successfully to begin a conversation about spiritual things.

I asked Lance, a skycap at an East Coast airport, to read through the Would You Like to Know God Personally? booklet while I gathered the luggage. When all the suitcases were accounted for, I asked him, "Which circle represents your life?" "The one on the left," Lance replied. "Which circle would you like to represent your life?" "The one on the right," he said resolutely. Within a few moments, Lance had discerned his standing with God, and realized that he wanted to receive Jesus Christ as his Lord and Savior. Together we stood aside from the airport bustle, and Lance received Christ.

Page 10:

A Suggested Prayer

One receives Christ by faith. Prayer, however, is a tangible way of expressing faith and of opening the door of one's life to Christ. The suggested prayer on this page contains several important acknowledgments and commitments on the part of the listener, so read through it carefully with him.

Then come the two most important questions you will ask during the entire witnessing opportunity:

"John, does this prayer express the desire of your heart?"

"Would you like to pray this prayer right now?"

Do not be shy at this point. This is where the listener needs your confident, calm leadership. When he says "yes," have him repeat the prayer after you, a phrase at a time. When you have finished praying together, take a moment to congratulate him, then say, "Now let me ask you a few questions just so you understand what has just happened."

Page 11:
Assurance of Salvation

Ask the questions at the top of page 11 to help the new believer comprehend the promises of God's Word. He can be assured, because God and His Word are reliable, that Christ is now in his life.

And, because God and His Word are trustworthy, he now has eternal life. Continue reading to affirm this.

Page 12:
You may not feel different

Page 12 addresses the question of feelings. Some people have dramatic conversions, while for others it's a calm, quiet decision. Continue reading through the text, emphasizing how the train diagram illustrates that we have faith in the fact of God's Word. Feelings are a result of our faith, not a cause of our faith. God's promises are based on His trustworthiness, not on how we feel.

Page 13:
Summary of the New Life

Page 13 is a quick overview of what transpired in the new believer's life when he received Christ. You'll want to encourage him to take the booklet home, open his Bible, and look up each reference in context to affirm that God has indeed worked a miracle of love in his life. If time allows, pray together as suggested at the bottom of the page, thanking God for what He has done.

Pages 14 & 15:
Growth Suggestions

Here is a mini-course on what to do to grow in a newfound relationship with Jesus Christ. Encourage the new believer to study these on his own too.

We strongly believe in, and are committed to serving, the local church. A new believer needs to find a fellowship of loving, committed Christians who love the Lord and His inspired Word, and who will encourage and strengthen his walk with God.

After the Presentation

I cannot stress enough the importance of follow-up for the new believer. If you live in close proximity, always make an appointment to get together within fourty-eight hours of his decision. He will likely have questions and perhaps will be wrestling with a variety of emotions, and you can help him get a solid footing for his new walk with God.

If the new believer is a casual encounter, commit yourself to conscientious mail and phone follow-up.

In either case, it is essential that you:

1. Exchange addresses, phone numbers and e-mail addresses.

2. Give him the booklet and encourage him to read through it again that night. It is also important that he begin to study the New Testament, beginning with the Gospel of John. Encourage him to read the first three chapters that night before going to bed.

3. If you live in close proximity, set up a personal appointment to meet again within 48 hours. If you don't live nearby, ask permission to call to "see how it's going."

Note: If the new believer is of the opposite sex, I strongly recommend that you have a trusted friend of the same gender do the follow-up. I have often told women, for example, "I know a Christian woman whose background is very similar to yours. Would you mind if I had her contact you?" This precaution can prevent potential misunderstandings and mixed up emotions.

Pulling it All Together

Let me encourage you to find a friend with whom you can practice using the booklet, to shake out the initial jitters you might feel as you begin to read through the booklet aloud. Have your friend be a "friendly listener" at this point, posing no objections or questions. The aim is to get you comfortable with the basic presentation.

Then pray and trust God to help you pass on the amazing news of what He has done for us.

Adapted from <u>Witnessing without Fear</u> by Bill Bright, Chapter 9

Small Group Hospitality Study & Discussion

What better place to use your newly acquired hospitality skills than in your home group or small group. Whether you attend a mega-church or not, many churches are now encouraging the formation of small groups to build a sense of community within the congregation. Challenge your small group to have an event. Everybody can bring an unchurched friend. To prepare your small group for this challenge, have them do the Bible study and discussion in this section.

My daughter shared with me how her women's small group happened upon this concept by accident. They decided to have a Girls Night Out social and the hostess brought her unchurched neighbor. The neighbor watched the evening unfold and joined in the conversation and laughter. At the end of the evening, she thanked them profusely for including her and remarked about how much fun they all had together. Then, wonder of wonders, she asked them if she could join their Bible study group! There are hundreds of men and women out there who would do the same if your small group would just try some of the events in this book.

What the Bible has to Say about
Hospitality

Knowing the Biblical basis for hospitality will show you how important it is to our Lord. Not only is it important to know why we do something, it is encouraging to see how simply it was done for thousands of years. The impact of hospitality is powerful — whether to a total stranger or an important government official. What's even more exciting is that the Lord Jesus Christ comes to all our events for he promises us that, "For where two or three come together in my name, there am I with them." Matthew 18:20 NIV. It's fun to imagine him standing in a corner of my home, watching and listening. We even have a framed drawing of our house that says that very thought. It hangs in our kitchen by the table.

I hope that when you meditate on these passages of scripture, you will see the Biblical basis for hospitality. Use these during your personal times with the Lord. Expand upon them with your small group or with your Bible study group. Who knows, Entertaining for Eternity with Heavenly Hospitality may become exciting and contagious!

You can use these passages and questions with your small group or Bible study. Would it be great to see a groundswell of hospitality resulting from this study? If church small groups would band together to begin having some of the various events mentioned in this book, the churches would begin to grow. Unchurched neighbors, co-workers and various associates in our lives are probably far more likely to respond to your group's hospitality event than to go to a church service. They often are unsure of what will be expected of them in a service. Large meetings are far less personal than hospitality in a home. That is how the church in the book of Acts operated. They did not even have a church building. And look at how that church grew and turned their known world upside down. Their homes were small and modest compared to ours today. This is how churches in China and in many third world countries world have to do things.

How the Unchurched Feel about Attending a Large Church Event

This was brought home to me one afternoon. I had taken a beginners painting class at the Michael's Craft store down the street from my home. The teacher was trying to encourage us to come to a luncheon that she was helping to sponsor at a local hotel. What motivated me to add this to my busy schedule was the possibility of winning a prize! There were going to be all sorts of small works of original art and crafts, hand-painted by local artists as well as by my teacher.

I decided also to invite my girlfriend who plans our church's annual Christmas craft night. I thought she would get some good ideas for her event.

I arrived at the hotel a little early and checked in at the luncheon table. I looked around the ballroom at the lovely craft and art display tables — still no girlfriend. As I stood waiting in the hall, I began to observe all the other ladies attending. They were all busy talking with each other about art. Clearly they all knew more about it than I did. They were asking each other questions and showing each other some of their work. It was beyond my amateur abilities to talk about.

I began to feel out of place. I continued to look for my friend so I would have someone to talk to. She was still not there. I stood closer to the hall leading out to the door of the hotel, straining for a glimpse of her. Then as I stood on the fringes of this group of artsy women, feeling alone, I began to notice that most of these women were either wearing some of their art in the form of painted jewelry or clothing or were carrying a hand-painted purse or something displaying their talents. I continued to feel left out and make trips to the hotel door.

Finally, my friend came rushing in from the parking lot. I hugged her, glad to have the company of someone more like me. We ended up having a lovely lunch together and chatted with the women at our table. I did not win a prize but my friend did.

I learned something valuable while waiting in that hallway. The Holy Spirit spoke to me that afternoon and said, "Now you know how a nonbeliever feels when they come to church for the first time or when they come to one of your events."

That has caused me to keep my eye out for visitors to Christian events and to do as much as I can to make them feel a part of things. I realize that we believers cannot stand around talking in our Christian jargon about things that nonbelievers may not understand. If you ever find yourself in a similar situation, do what you can to disengage your Christian friends from their oblivion and do what you can to change the conversation to something that nonbelievers can engage in. Remember it's all about them and not about us!

Biblical Basis Scriptures

In Romans 12:13 NIV we read, "Practice hospitality." The word hospitality comes from two Greek words: philos meaning loving, and xenos meaning strangers. This biblical meaning transcends our modern definition of entertaining friends. It means to treat strangers in a way that they know they are loved, like part of a family. Hospitality dates as far back as Genesis, the first book of the Bible. Abraham, the father of Judaism, was the first to show us how to be hospitable when three strangers came to him.

Genesis 18:2-8 NIV
"Abraham looked up and saw three men standing nearby. When he saw them, he hurried from the entrance of his tent to meet them and bowed low to the ground. He said, "If I have found favor in your eyes, my lord, do not pass your servant by. Let a little water be brought, and then you may all wash your feet and rest under this tree. Let me get you something to eat, so you can be refreshed and then go on your way—now that you have come to your servant." "Very well," they answered, "do as you say."

So Abraham hurried into the tent to Sarah. "Quick," he said, "Get three seahs of fine flour and knead it and bake some bread." Then he ran to the herd and selected a choice, tender calf and gave it to a servant, who hurried to prepare it. He then brought some curds and milk and the calf that had been prepared, and set these before them. While they ate, he stood near them under a tree."

Scriptures give us many other examples of hospitality. There is no doubt that this should be a vital part of every believer's life whether or not they have the "gift of hospitality." We should offer hospitality to more than just our family and good friends. We have a special responsibility to all believers and especially to those who are in full-time service for the Lord. 3 John 1:8 NIV "We ought therefore to show hospitality to such men so that we may work together for the truth."

The emphasis of this book, however, is on reaching out to those who may not know Jesus Christ in a personal way. Those without Christ are very needy in many ways. We are also supposed to show hospitality to the poor and even to our "enemies", not just to those who are our friends. Remember what it says in Hebrews 13:1-3, 16 NIV "Keep on loving each other as brothers. Do not forget to entertain strangers, for by so doing some people have entertained angels without knowing it. Remember those in prison as if you were their fellow-prisoners, and those who are ill-treated as if you yourselves were suffering...And do not forget to do good and to share with others, for with such sacrifices God is pleased."

Matthew 5:43-47 NIV says, "You have heard that it was said, 'Love your neighbor and hate your enemy' but I tell you: Love your enemies and pray for those who persecute you, that you may be sons of your Father in heaven. He causes his sun to rise on the evil and the good, and sends rain on the righteous and the unrighteous. If you love those who love you, what reward will you get? Are not even the tax collectors doing that? And if you greet only your brothers, what are you doing more than others? Do not even pagans do that?"

Paul told the new believers in Rome, "Share with God's people who are in need. Practice hospitality." Romans 12:13 NIV

Mary and Martha were excellent New Testament examples of how to show hospitality. They often took care of Jesus and his disciples. Martha eagerly opened her home. Mary showed us how to make sure that we do not get bogged down in the details and miss the key element of connecting with our guests. Both women had something significant to offer.

We see this in Luke 10:38-42 NIV also. "As Jesus and his disciples were on their way, he came to a village where a woman named Martha opened her home to him. She had a sister called Mary, who sat at the Lord's feet listening to what he said. But Martha was distracted by all the preparations that had to be made. She came to him and asked, 'Lord, do you not care that my sister has left me to do the work by myself? Tell her to help me!' 'Martha, Martha,' the Lord answered, 'you are worried and upset about many things, but only one thing is needed. Mary has chosen what is better, and it will not be taken away from her.'"

In the New Testament, one of the requirements for church leaders is that they show hospitality. I Timothy 3:2 and Titus 1:8 list hospitality as one of the traits that they should demonstrate. Paul talks about it in Acts 28:7, praising a man named Publius, a chief official on Malta who opened his estate to Paul and allowed him to minister there. He entertained Paul and his entourage for three days. That was quite a guest list! In Romans 16:23 Paul praises Gaius for how he showed hospitality to the whole church.

Both Peter and Paul included hospitality in their teachings on love. In Romans 12:16 NIV Paul adds "showing hospitality" to a long list of characteristics that all believers should have. In I Peter 4:9 NIV, Peter says, "Be hospitable to one another without complaint." As a matter of fact the nonbelievers in Acts were amazed at how much they saw hospitality demonstrated by the believers! It was something that impressed them and made Christianity attractive to them. Oh, that our neighbors would notice that about us.

Acts 2:42-47 NIV "They devoted themselves to the apostles' teaching and to the fellowship to the breaking of bread and to prayer. Everyone was filled with awe, and many wonders and miraculous signs were done by the apostles. All the believers were together and had everything in common. Selling their possessions and goods, they gave to anyone as he had need. Every day they continued to meet together in the temple courts. They broke bread in their homes and ate together with glad and sincere hearts, praising God and enjoying the favor of all the people. And the Lord added to their number daily those who were being saved."

Often we fall into the trap of believing that our homes have to be perfect, our dishes all have to match or that we need to be gourmet cooks in order to entertain guests. Yet, hospitality is a means to use our gifts to serve others. It should be "offered" despite limited financial means or our busy schedules. There are many ways we can "offer hospitality" to others, and we should we be looking for ways to serve not only our close friends and relatives, but also anyone in need. Pray for opportunities to offer hospitality, and God will equip you to serve! Consider the Proverbs 31 woman, "she opens her arms to the poor and extends her hands to the needy" (NIV).

Biblical Basis Discussion Questions

- What does the word hospitality really mean?
- In Genesis 18:2-8, what was the first thing that Abraham did when he had guests? What did that communicate?
- What did it mean to wash feet in Abraham's day and what would be something equivalent in our day?
- Why is food such a vital part of hospitality?
- Abraham refers to himself as "your servant." What kind of attitude does that reveal?
- When Sarah got involved, what kind and quality of preparations were made?
- Read III John 1:8. Why is it important to show hospitality to those who are in "full time service" for the Lord?
- What might be the particular needs of a Christian worker?
- According to Hebrews 13:13 and 16, to whom should we show hospitality?
- What interesting guests may be at our table or in our home without us even realizing it?
- According to Matthew 5:43-47, what unlikely guests should we entertain? Why?
- What category of guests are mentioned in Romans 12:13?
- Jesus often stayed in the home of what two women and what two different approaches did they take? Why were both important parts of hospitality?
- Which approach do you tend to gravitate toward and how can you add some of the other approach to your style?
- Why do you think showing hospitality is a prerequisite for being a church leader in I Timothy 3:2, Titus 1:8 and Acts 28:7?
- What did the couple in II Kings 4:8-13 do and for whom did they do it? What did they want in return?
- Having house guests is a bigger commitment. Who else role modeled this and to whom in Acts 28:7? How long did all these people stay?
- What did Gaius do in Romans 16:23?
- How does I Peter 4:9 tell us to show hospitality?
- What do we want our neighbors to notice about us that the unbelievers in Acts saw?
- What was the result of Acts 2:42-47 among the observing unbelievers?

Following Up Decisions for Christ

Contact those who have indicated decisions for Christ within a week after your event or when you last met with them. Seek to meet them for coffee briefly. At the coffee review the "Would You Like to Know Christ Personally" booklet and stress the importance of growing spiritually through Bible study. Offer to help them if you are not planning a follow-up Bible study or discussion.

There are many Bible study materials available to follow-up decisions for Christ. The most effective are best used in a personal manner, rather than trusting the individual to get started in their walk with the Lord on their own. Individual and small group studies work with any of the following materials. It is best not to ask them to make a long-term commitment for your meetings. Suggest meeting with them for a few weeks to start. Tell them that they do not need any prior Biblical knowledge and, if needed, you can get them a Bible. Choose one of the modern versions to get them started. Pick a time that is most convenient for them.

Bible study suggestions

- Five Steps to Christian Growth (Campus Crusade for Christ) - a five week study
- Ten Basic Steps to Christian Growth by Bill Bright. Use the Introductory or Step 1 from this series.
- The Gospel of John from the New Testament. Use some of the questions in the margins of the Quest Bible (Zondervan Press)
- Growing in Christ (Nav Press) which is 13 weeks long.
- Jesus Cares for Women (Nav Press) by Helen Ashker
- Life Guide Bible Studies (InterVarsity Press) on various individual topics
- Seeker Studies (InterVarsity Press) any of the following titles;
- Encountering Jesus, Meeting Jesus, Jesus - The Reason

For Help Answering Tough Questions Regarding Faith

Books

Know Why You Believe by Paul Little

The Case for Christ and The Case for Faith by Lee Stroebel

Websites

www.EvidenceofGod.com

www.apologetics.com

www.leaderU.com

All of these recipes are not only delicious and memorable, but can be prepared well in advance. This will allow you more time to focus on your guests when they arrive. For large crowds, simply double or triple the recipes. Casserole type recipes should be made in single batches.

Breakfast or Brunch

Batter Bread

1 pkg. yeast
1 1/4 c. lukewarm water
2 Tbsp. honey
2 Tbsp. butter, softened
1 tsp. salt
3 c. flour, divided
Optional:
1 Tbsp. cinnamon
1 c. raisins

Dissolve yeast in water. Stir in honey. Add in butter, salt, and 2 c. flour. Beat well. Stir in remaining cup of flour until smooth. Cover and let rise until doubled, about 1 hour.

For optional cinnamon raisin bread: after rising, add in cinnamon and raisins.

Prepare 1 loaf pan with cooking spray. Let rise again until doubled in size.

Bake at 375 degrees for 35-40 minutes. Makes 1 loaf.

Butterscotch Rolls

1 pkg. frozen dinner roll dough (like Rich's), thawed for 30 minutes
1 c. chopped nuts
1 apple, peeled and cubed
1/2 c. raisins
1 pkg. cook and serve butterscotch pudding
1/2 c. butter, melted
1/2 c. brown sugar

Prepare Bundt pan with cooking spray. Cover the bottom of the Bundt pan with chopped nuts. Next, add dinner roll dough to the pan. Add in apples and raisins. Sprinkle on butterscotch pudding mix, then drizzle with melted butter and brown sugar. Let rise until doubled in size.

Bake at 375 degrees for 25-30 minutes. Turn out on large serving plate.

Blueberry Coffee Cake

*This can be made ahead and refrigerated overnight before baking.
1/2 c. brown sugar
1/2 tsp. ground cinnamon
1 – 12 oz. can home style refrigerated buttermilk biscuits
1/4 c. butter, melted
1 c. quick-cooking oats
1 1/2 c. fresh or frozen blueberries
1/4 c. sugar
2 Tbsp. butter, cut into small pieces

Preheat oven to 375 degrees. Prepare an 8 or 9-inch square baking dish with cooking spray. In small bowl, mix brown sugar and cinnamon.

Separate dough into individual biscuits. Cut each biscuit into quarters. Dip each piece in melted butter and coat with brown sugar mixture. Arrange in a single layer in baking dish. Sprinkle with 1/2 c. of oats.

In medium bowl, toss blueberries and sugar until coated. Spoon over biscuits and oats. Sprinkle with remaining 1/2 c. of oats. Dot with butter pieces.

Bake for 30-35 minutes or until golden brown around the edges and center is done. Cool for 20 minutes before serving.

Cream Scones

2 c. flour
2 Tbsp. sugar
1 Tbsp. baking powder
1 tsp. salt
1/3 c. currants or raisins (optional)
1 1/4 c. heavy cream
1/4 c. sour cream
1 c. heavy whipping cream
1 drop yellow food coloring

Preheat oven to 425 degrees. Combine flour, sugar, baking powder, salt and currants or raisins. Add cream and mix until well blended, but sticky. Press together gently to form a ball then knead 4 to 5 times. Roll out on floured surface to 1/2 inch thick. Cut into 1-2 inch rounds. Place on ungreased baking sheet, no more than 1/2-inch apart. Brush with heavy cream and sprinkle with sugar. Bake for 10-14 minutes, depending on size of scones. Cool slightly. Serve warm with jams or cream.

To make cream: beat heavy whipping cream and food coloring until very stiff (will almost turn to butter). Gradually blend in sour cream. Serve on warm scones.

Easy Blender Fruit Smoothie

1 apple
1 orange
1 banana
1/2 c. frozen strawberries
1 c. any fruit juice, cranberry or orange
Optional garnish: whipped cream

Prepare fruit by cutting into large chunks. Blend all ingredients on low first, then gradually turn blender to highest speed. Blend until smooth. Serve in small glasses with garnish of whipped cream.

Easy Egg Casserole

12 slices of buttered bread with crusts removed
1 lb. fresh sausage, lightly browned
1/2 lb. shredded cheese
6 eggs
3 c. milk

Place 6 slices of bread in 3 qt. casserole dish with buttered side up. Spread half of the sausage and half of the cheese on top of bread. Make a second layer with the remaining sausage and cheese. Lightly beat eggs and milk and pour over casserole pressing down the bread until the milk comes through. Refrigerate overnight. Bake uncovered at 350 degrees for 1 hour.

Easy Quiche

1 store bought frozen pie shell
3 eggs
1 1/2 c. milk
1 1/2 c. shredded cheese
1 c. vegetables or meat *
*Use any vegetable or meat of your choice: broccoli, asparagus, mushrooms, zucchini, shrimp, crab, bacon, sausage, ground beef, chicken, tuna, etc.

Bake pie shell at 450 degrees for 5 minutes.

Whisk together eggs and milk. Stir in cheese, vegetables and meat of your choice. Pour egg mixture into pie shell and bake at 375 degrees for 50 minutes.

Tip

The egg mixture can be prepared ahead of time and poured into the pie shell immediately before baking.

Overnight Apple French Toast

1 c. brown sugar
1/2 c. butter, melted
2 Tbsp. light corn syrup
3 tsp. ground cinnamon, separated
1/4 c. dried cranberries or raisins
3 apples, peeled and cut into ¼ inch slices
6 eggs
1 1/2 c. milk
1 tsp. vanilla extract
1 loaf day old French bread, cut into slices

Prepare 9 x 13 pan with cooking spray. Combine brown sugar, butter, corn syrup, 1 tsp. cinnamon, and 1/4 c. dried cranberries or raisins. Set aside. In separate bowl, beat together eggs, milk, vanilla, and 2 tsp. cinnamon.

Layer in 9x13 pan, apples slices, brown sugar mixture, slices of French bread, and lastly, egg mixture (soaking bread completely). Cover and refrigerate for at least 4 hours or overnight.

Remove from refrigerator 30 minutes before baking. Bake uncovered at 350 degrees for 35-40 minutes.

For optional syrup topping:

Combine and heat 1 c. applesauce, 1 -10 oz. jar of apple or apricot jelly, ½ tsp. cinnamon, and 1/8 tsp. ground cloves.

Baked Brie with Apples and Cranberries

1/2 c. apples, chopped
1/4 c. sliced almonds
1/4 c. dried cranberries
1 Tbsp. brown sugar
1/4 tsp. cinnamon
1 Tbsp. melted butter
1 – 8 oz. round of Brie cheese
Crackers for serving

Preheat oven to 350 degrees. Combine apples, almonds, cranberries, brown sugar, and cinnamon; mix gently. Stir in butter just until moistened.

Cut Brie in half horizontally. Place one half, rind side down, in baking dish. Spoon half of apple mixture onto Brie and spread evenly. Top with remaining half of Brie, rind side up. Spoon remaining apple mixture over top. Bake for 12-15 minutes or until cheese is soft and just beginning to melt. Serve warm with crackers.

Big Game Cheese Dip

1 block of Velveeta cheese
1 lb. pork sausage, cooked and drained well
1 can Hormel with chilies
Tortilla chips for serving

Combine cheese, sausage, and chilies in crock pot and heat until thoroughly melted together. Serve with tortilla chips or vegetables for dipping.

Easy Cheese Ring

1 lb. finely shredded sharp cheddar cheese
1 c. mayonnaise
1 c. pecans, chopped
1/2 c. onion, finely chopped
Freshly ground pepper
Dash of cayenne pepper
12 oz. strawberry preserves
Whole wheat crackers for serving

In medium bowl, combine cheese, mayonnaise, pecans, and onions. Add pepper and cayenne and blend thoroughly. Press mixture into a 3 c. mold or form into a ring on serving plate. Refrigerate for at least 2 hours. Fill center of ring with strawberry preserves and serve with crackers.

Healthy Chicken Salad Dip

2 Tbsp. nonfat plain yogurt
2 Tbsp. light mayonnaise
1/3 c. chopped celery
2 Tbsp. finely chopped onion
1 – 9.75 oz. can chuck chicken breast, drained
Salt & pepper
Whole wheat bread or crackers for serving

Combine yogurt, mayonnaise, celery, onion, and chicken in bowl. Add salt and pepper to taste. Serve on bread as finger sandwiches or in a bowl with crackers as a dip.

Quick & Easy Meatballs

1 lb. pork sausage, cooked and drained well
1 1/2 c. baking mix, such as Bisquick
2-3 c. shredded cheddar cheese
1 egg

Preheat oven to 350 degrees. Combine all ingredients in a large mixing bowl. Form into balls using your hands. Place on ungreased cookie sheet and bake for 15 minutes. Flip meatballs and bake another 10-15 minutes or until golden brown. Baking time varies depending on size of meatballs.

Spinach Dip

1 pkg. frozen chopped spinach, thawed and drained well
1 c. mayonnaise
1 c. sour cream
1 medium onion, finely chopped
1 - 8 oz. can of water chestnuts, chopped
1 pkg. dehydrated vegetable soup mix, such as Knorr
1/4 c. Parmesan cheese
1 loaf sour dough bread

Combine ingredients and serve in large sour dough bread bowl. To make bread bowl, hollow out a round loaf of sour dough bread. Cube the hollowed bread and use for dipping.

Taco Dip

1 large can refried beans
1 tub of store bought guacamole dip
1/2 c. sour cream
1/2 c. mayonnaise
1/2 packet of taco seasoning
2 tomatoes, seeded and diced
1 can black olives, drained
1-2 c. finely shredded cheddar or Mexican blend cheese
Tortilla chips for serving

Combine sour cream, mayonnaise, and taco seasoning. Blend well.

In 8-9 inch pie pan, layer refried beans, guacamole dip, and sour cream mixture. Top with diced tomatoes, black olives, and shredded cheese. Chill in refrigerator until serving.

Barley Salad

2 c. hulled barley
2 Tbsp. unsalted butter
2 tsp. kosher salt
4 c. boiling water
3 Tbsp. orange juice
2 Tbsp. olive oil
1/4 c. pine nuts, toasted
1/2 c. Parmesan cheese
1/2 c. crumbled cooked bacon, about 5-6 slices
2 Tbsp. chopped fresh parsley
Freshly ground pepper

Prepare oven to 375 degrees. Place barley into a 1 ½ quart baking dish (with a lid) and add butter, salt and boiling water. Stir to combine. Cover the dish tightly with foil and place lid on top of foil. Bake on the middle rack of the oven for 1 hour. After 1 hour, remove cover, fluff with a fork and cool.

In a small bowl, whisk together the orange juice and a pinch of kosher salt. Add the olive oil and whisk to combine to make a dressing. Set aside.

Combine the barley, pine nuts, Parmesan cheese, bacon and parsley in a large mixing bowl. Add the dressing and stir to combine. Season, to taste, with salt and pepper. Serve warm as a main dish or cold as a side dish.

Broccoli Salad

1 head of broccoli
1/4 c. raisins
1 small red onion, sliced
1 c. mayonnaise
1/4 c. sugar
2 Tbsp. vinegar
8 slices of crisp bacon, crumbled

Combine mayonnaise, sugar, and vinegar to make a dressing. Toss broccoli, raisins, red onion, and bacon with dressing. Chill before serving.

Broccoli Slaw

4 Tbsp. sugar
1/8 tsp. seasoned salt
6 Tbsp. rice vinegar
1 tsp. salt
1 pkg. broccoli slaw
6 green onions, finely chopped
1/2 c. sliced almonds
1/2 c. sunflower seeds
2 pkgs. Ramen noodles, broken into small pieces, flavoring discarded

Whisk together sugar, vinegar, and salts. Combine broccoli slaw and green onions in large bowl. Pour dressing mixture over broccoli slaw and refrigerate overnight. Just before serving, add almonds, sunflower seeds, and noodles.

Individual Quick Salad Ideas

Top a bed of lettuce with various salad ingredients. For example:
Mandarin orange slices
Dried cranberries or raisins
Almond slivers
Carrots
Green Onions
Tomatoes, chopped

Drizzle with favorite dressing such as poppy seed, or have several different dressings available for guests to choose from.

Mandarin Salad

½ tsp. salt
¼ tsp. pepper
3 Tbsp. sugar, divided
2 Tbsp. salad vinegar
1/4 c. vegetable oil
1 Tbsp. parsley
1/4 c. sliced almonds
1 Tbsp. butter
Romaine lettuce
2 stalks of celery, finely chopped
1 bunch of green onions, finely chopped
1 can mandarin orange, drained
1 c. red grapes, cut in half

Combine salt, pepper, 2 Tbsp. sugar, vinegar, oil, and parsley and whisk until well blended. Store in air tight container in refrigerator for several hours or overnight to allow flavors to blend.

In small non-stick skillet, melt butter and 1 Tbsp. sugar until caramel in color. Stir in slivered almonds and toast until golden brown.

Make salad of lettuce, chopped celery, green onions, mandarin oranges, and grapes. Drizzle on dressing and top with caramelized almonds.

Summer Vegetable Salad with Lemon Vinaigrette

1 lb. asparagus, cut into bite-size pieces
2 c. grape or cherry tomatoes, cut in half
1 bunch broccoli, cut into bite-size pieces
1 yellow pepper, chopped
1 red pepper, chopped
1 tsp. grated lemon peel
2 Tbsp. fresh lemon juice
1 Tbsp. fresh thyme or ¼ tsp. ground thyme
2 tsp. brown sugar
1 tsp. salt
1 tsp. Dijon mustard
Fresh ground pepper
3 Tbsp. extra virgin olive oil

Whisk together lemon juice and peel, thyme, brown sugar, salt, mustard, and pepper. Whisk vigorously and slowly drizzle in olive oil in a steady stream, continue whisking until well blended.

Place asparagus and broccoli in large microwavable bowl. Heat in microwave on high for 2 minutes or until slightly tender. Add other vegetables and drizzle on vinaigrette and toss to coat. Chill and cover for a few hours before serving.

Vegetable Marinade

4 stalks of fresh broccoli, broken up
8 large fresh mushrooms, sliced
1 medium green pepper, chopped
3 stalks of celery, chopped
1 small cauliflower, broken up
2/3 c. sugar
2 tsp. dry mustard
1 tsp. salt
1/2 c. vinegar
3/4 c. oil
1 small onion, minced
2 Tbsp. poppy seeds

Chop and slice all vegetables. Combine in a large bowl. In medium bowl, whisk together sugar, dry mustard, salt, vinegar, oil, minced onion, and poppy seeds. Toss vegetables in dressing and chill at least 3 hours.

Tip

This is a great summer time dish that goes well with a shrimp boil and roasted potatoes.

Asian Chicken & Rice Buffet

Whether you are providing all of the food, or everyone is pitching in and bringing an item, this is great for serving a large crowd. Arrange items in order as shown in recipe on long table or counter. For dessert, serve Chinese fortune cookies and hot tea.

Steamed rice
Stewed chicken with cream of chicken soup
Crispy Chow Mien noodles
Green onions, finely chopped
Celery, chopped
Shredded cheddar cheese
Mandarin oranges
Crushed pineapple
Shredded coconut
Almonds and peanuts

Basic Pot Roasts

3-4 lb. rump roast
2-3 potatoes, peeled and chopped
2-3 large carrots; peeled and chopped
1-2 onions, peeled and sliced
1 c. beef broth
Salt & pepper to taste
2-3 tsp. cornstarch

Place all vegetables in bottom of crock pot. Salt and pepper the meat and place on top of the vegetables. Pour beef broth over meat and vegetables. Cook on low for 10-12 hours, on high for 4-5 hours. Remove meat and vegetables and thicken broth with 2-3 tsp. cornstarch.

Variations:

French style – Omit carrots and potatoes and add 1 c. fresh mushrooms or 8 oz. can of mushrooms. Replace beef broth with 1 c. red wine.

Italian style – Add 1 – 8 oz. can of tomato sauce, 1 tsp. oregano and 1 tsp. basil to roast.

Chicken au Gratin

20 pieces of chicken
Paprika
8 diced green onions
1 red pepper, chopped (optional)
4 c. shredded cheddar cheese
2 cans cream of chicken or mushroom soup
1/4 c. white cooking wine
1 pint sour cream
Steamed rice for serving

Preheat oven to 325 degrees. Prepare two 9x13 baking dishes with cooking spray. Place chicken in baking dishes and sprinkle with paprika. Next, sprinkle with cheese and green onions. Combine soups, wine, and sour cream and pour over chicken. Bake uncovered for 1 ¼ hours. To serve, move chicken to serving platter and serve sauce in a gravy boat. Serve over rice.

Chicken Elegant

6 large cooked chicken breasts, cut into large chunks
1 pint sour cream
1 can mushroom caps
1 can cream of mushroom soup
1/4 lb. butter
1 c. chicken broth
1 pkg. herb stuffing mix

Preheat oven to 350 degrees. Combine chicken chunks, sour cream, mushrooms, and mushroom soup. Spread in 9x13 baking dish.

Heat chicken broth and butter until melted. Stir into herb stuffing mix. Spread stuffing over chicken mixture. Bake for 45 minutes or until bubbly.

Chicken Pilaf

1 1/3 c. dry instant rice
4-6 c. cooked chicken chunks
1 can mushroom soup
1 1/4 c. boiling water
1/2 envelope of dehydrated onion soup mix
1/4 c. cooking sherry

Preheat oven to 375 degrees. In 9x13 baking dish, put instant rice and top with chunks of chicken. Mix together mushroom soup, boiling water, onion soup mix, and sherry. Pour over chicken and rice. Cover and bake for 1 ¼ hours.

Chicken Saltimbocca

4 large chicken breasts
6 thin slices of prosciutto or boiled ham
4 slices of mozzarella cheese
1 medium tomato, thinly sliced
2 bunches of fresh sage, minced
1/2 c. dry bread crumbs
2 Tbsp. Parmesan cheese
2 Tbsp. parsley
4 Tbsp. melted butter

Preheat oven to 350 degrees. Prepare a 9x13 baking dish with cooking spray. Pound chicken breasts and flatten to a size of approximately 5x5 inches. On each piece of chicken, layer prosciutto, cheese, tomato slices, and sprinkle on minced sage. Roll each and sell well.

Combine bread crumbs, parsley, and Parmesan cheese. Dip each chicken roll in melted butter and then roll in bread crumb mixture. Place seam side down in baking dish and bake for 40-45 minutes.

Company Chicken Casserole

4-6 c. cooked chicken chunks
1 pkg. frozen green beans, cooked and drained
1 can of mushroom soup
1 can sliced water chestnuts
1 can sliced mushrooms
1/2 c. grated Parmesan cheese
1/4 c. cooking sherry
1 can fried onions

Preheat oven to 350 degrees. Combine chicken, green beans, mushroom soup, water chestnuts, mushrooms, and Parmesan cheese. Spread in 9x13 baking dish. Splash with cooking sherry. Bake for 25 minutes. Top with fried onions and bake an additional 5 minutes.

Crock Pot Barbecue Beef Stew

2 lbs. beef stew meat, cut in 1 inch pieces
2 Tbsp. cooking oil
1 c. thinly sliced onion rings
1/2 c. green pepper, chopped
1 large garlic clove, minced
1/2 tsp. salt
2 c. beef broth
1 - 8 oz. can of tomatoes, chopped, juices reserved
1 – 4 oz. can of mushrooms
1/3 c. bottled barbecue sauce
1/4 c. cold water
3 Tbsp. cornstarch
Steamed rice for serving

In large non-stick skillet, brown meat in oil. Drain. Place onion rings, green pepper and garlic in crock pot. Place meat on top and sprinkle with salt and freshly ground pepper. Add beef broth, tomatoes and their juices, mushrooms, and barbecue sauce and cover. Cook on low for 8-10 hours.

Combine cold water and cornstarch and stir into stew. Cook until thickened and bubbly, stirring occasionally.

Serve over steamed rice. Serves 6-8.

Easy Oven Barbecue Brisket

1/4 - 1/2 lb. beef brisket per person, fat removed
1 large bottle of your favorite barbecue sauce
Salt, pepper, and garlic salt for seasoning
Hamburger buns for serving

Preheat oven to 250 degrees. Prepare a 9x13 baking dish with cooking spray.

Sprinkle meat on all sides with salt, pepper, and garlic salt.

Bake for 8-10 hours. Drain off most of the grease and slice very thin and return to baking dish. Heat barbecue sauce in microwave and pour over the meat.

Option:

Serve with or without buns. Meat will go further when served with buns.

Easy Oven Fried Chicken

2-2 1/2 lbs. of chicken pieces
1/2 c. flour
1 tsp. salt
1/4 tsp. pepper
1/4 tsp. paprika
1/4 c. melted shortening

Preheat oven to 425 degrees. Combine flour, salt, pepper, and paprika. Place flour mixture and chicken in large zip top bag and shake to coat. Add melted shortening to a 9x13 baking dish. Place chicken, in a single layer, skin side down. Bake for 40 minutes. Turn chicken over and bake another 10 minutes until chicken is crispy.

Tip:

Great for crowds and picnics, just double or triple for appropriate amount.

Hot Chicken Salad

1 c. slivered almonds
3 c. cooked chicken
2 c. chopped celery
2 3/4 c. mayonnaise
1 c. shredded Colby cheese
2 Tbsp. chopped onion
3 tsp. lemon juice
½ tsp. salt
½ tsp. pepper
½ c. cracker crumbs, crushed

Preheat oven to 375 degrees. Prepare 9x13 pan with cooking spray. Combine almonds and cracker crumbs and set aside. Combine chicken, celery, mayonnaise, cheese, onion, lemon juice, salt, and pepper. Place chicken mixed into baking dish and top with almond and cracker mixture. Bake for 15-20 minutes.

Crockpot Corned Beef

1 orange, washed (for zest and juice)
1/2 cup apple juice
2 Tablespoons brown sugar, packed
2 teaspoons prepared yellow mustard
6 whole cloves
2 medium sweet onions, sliced thick
1 large Idaho potato, peeled and sliced thick
2-1/2 to 3 pounds corned beef brisket, trimmed of fat, rinsed, and patted dry
1 head green cabbage, cut into 8 wedges

Using a grater, remove and reserve the zest from the orange. Cut the orange in half and juice it into a medium bowl. To the orange zest and juice, add apple juice, brown sugar, mustard, and cloves. Whisk to combine and set aside.

Layer onions in the bottom of a large oval crockpot and top with the potato slices. Place corned beef on top. Pour the apple mixture evenly over the top of the corned beef. Arrange cabbage wedges on top of the meat. Cover and cook on Low for 8 hours or on High for 5 to 6 hours.

Remove corned beef to a platter, cover with foil, and let rest for 15 minutes before slicing across the grain to serve.

Freezer Lasagna

2 lbs. ground beef or turkey
1 large can diced tomatoes
1 medium can tomato sauce
1 small can tomato paste
3 Tbsp. parsley
1 tsp. basil
Salt & pepper to taste
1 tsp. garlic powder
2 c. cottage cheese
2 eggs
1/2 c. Parmesan cheese
10 -12 lasagna noodles
2 lbs. mozzarella cheese, shredded

Cook ground beef in skillet and drain. In bowl, combine all tomatoes, 1 Tbsp. parsley, basil, salt, pepper, and garlic powder. Add tomato mixture to ground beef in skillet and simmer for 20 minutes. Cook lasagna noodles.

In another bowl, combine cottage cheese, eggs, 2 Tbsp. parsley, and Parmesan cheese.

Layer in 9x13 pan starting with noodles, then cottage cheese mixture, mozzarella cheese, and then meat and tomato mixture. Repeat layering. More layers can be done if space allows.

If serving immediately, bake at 375 degrees for 1 hour. Let cool a little before serving to allow to set. If freezing, cover tightly with plastic wrap, then foil and freeze for up to 2 weeks. Allow to thaw before baking, then follow directions as above.

Marinated Pork Chops

4 pork chops
1/4 c. soy sauce
1/4 c. teriyaki sauce
1 tsp. ginger
1 Tbsp. grated orange peel or lemon juice
2 Tbsp. green pepper or minced onion
1/4 c. pineapple juice
1/3 c. orange juice
1/3 c. oil
2 Tbsp. brown sugar

Combine all in small bowl. Place pork chops in baking dish and pour marinade over meat. Cover and refrigerate for at least 3-4 hours. Baste with marinade while grilling.

Pot Luck Pasta Bar

Another great idea for large groups. Invite everyone to bring one item such as cooked pasta, a sauce, a bowl of shredded cheese, or any pasta topping. Guests can also bring side items such as salad, bread, or a dessert. Below is a list of suggested items one might serve.

2-3 types of cooked pasta
Whole wheat pasta
Marinara sauce
Alfredo sauce
Pesto sauce
Meatballs
Chopped tomatoes
Steamed broccoli
Shredded chicken
Cooked shrimp
2 types of shredded cheese for topping (i.e. Parmesan, Asiago)

Savory Chicken Squares

1 – 3 oz. pkg. cream cheese, softened
2 Tbsp. milk
3 Tbsp. butter
2 c. cooked chicken, cubed
1/4 tsp. salt
1/8 tsp. pepper
1 Tbsp. pimento
1 Tbsp. chopped green onions
1 – 8 oz. pkg. refrigerated crescent rolls
¾ c. seasoned croutons crushed or bread crumbs

Preheat oven to 350 degrees.

Combine cream cheese, milk, and 2 Tbsp. butter and blend until smooth. Add chicken, salt, pepper, pimento, and green onions and mix well.

Tip:

This step can be done ahead of time and refrigerated until ready to bake.

Separate dough into 4 rectangles. Press perforations together to seal well. Spoon ½ c. chicken mixture into center of each rectangle. Pull 4 corners of dough up to the top center of mixture, seal by twisting slightly to make a pocket. Brush tops with 1 Tbsp. melted butter. Sprinkle bread crumbs over top. Bake on ungreased cookie sheet for 20-25 minutes until golden brown.

Tip:

Serve with the Mandarin Salad for a great luncheon.

Sour Cream Noodle Bake

1 – 8 oz. pkg. medium noodles
1 lb. lean ground beef
1 Tbsp. butter
1 tsp. salt
1/8 tsp. pepper
1/4 tsp. garlic salt
1 c. tomato sauce
1 c. creamed cottage cheese
1 c. sour cream
1 c. green onions, chopped
1 c. shredded sharp cheddar cheese

Preheat oven to 350 degrees. Cook noodles in boiling salted water. Rinse in cold water and drain. Brown beef in butter, drain, then add salt, pepper, garlic salt and tomato sauce. Simmer for 5 minutes.

Combine cottage cheese, sour cream, onions, and noodles. Alternate layers of noodle mixture and meat mixture in a 2-quart casserole dish, beginning with noodles and ending with meat. Top with shredded cheese. Bake for 20-25 minutes or until cheese is melted and slightly browned.

Tip:

For a healthier option, used reduced fat or light versions of cottage cheese, sour cream, and cheese.

Cherry Chip Cake Cookies

1 box of cherry chip cake mix
2 eggs
1/2 c. vegetable oil
1/2 c. powdered sugar

Preheat oven to 350 degrees. Combine cake mix, eggs, and oil. Mix well. Form dough in small balls and roll in powdered sugar. Place on parchment lined cookie sheets and bake for 8-10 minutes, do not over cook. Allow to cool 10-15 minutes on cookie sheet, then move to wire rack to cool completely.

Tip:

This is a great last minute recipe that can be made with any flavor of cake mix. Also great with chocolate, vanilla, or lemon cake mixes.

Chocolate Chip Bars

1 c. butter
3/4 c. sugar
3/4 c. brown sugar
1 tsp. vanilla
2 eggs
2 1/4 c. flour
1 tsp. baking soda
12 oz. chocolate chips
1 c. chopped nuts

Preheat oven to 375 degrees. Combine butter, sugars, and vanilla and beat well. Beat in eggs. Add in flour, baking soda, and salt. Stir in chocolate chips and nuts. Spread in 9x13 pan and bake for 25-30 minutes.

Cookie Cutter Cookies

1 c. shortening
2/3 c. sugar
2 eggs
2 tsp. vanilla
3/4 c. flour

Preheat oven to 350 degrees. Combine shortening, sugar, eggs, and vanilla. Stir in flour last. At this point, dough can be chilled to roll out later.

Roll dough out onto flour surface, using floured rolling pin, to approximately 1/4 inch thick and cut into shapes. Bake for 12-15 minutes.

Easy Cake with Chocolate Syrup & Berries

1 store bought pound cake or Angel food cake
1 jar of chocolate topping
1 pint of fresh sliced strawberries and/or blueberries
Whipped cream

Serve slices of pound cake or Angel food cake and drizzle with chocolate sauce. Top with sliced strawberries and/or blueberries and a dollop of whipped cream.

Fast Fixin' Chocolate Chip Cake

1 pkg. chocolate cake mix
1/4 c. oil
2 eggs
1 ¼ c. water
1 bag chocolate chips

Preheat oven to 350 degrees. Pour oil into 9x13 pan. Tilt pan until bottom is covered with oil. Add chocolate cake mix, eggs, and water into the pan and stir with a fork until well blended, about 2 minutes. Scrape sides, fold in chocolate chips, and spread evenly in pan. Bake for 35-40 minutes. Once cooled, sprinkle with powdered sugar.

Tip:

Place a paper doily over cooled cake and sprinkle with powdered sugar for a fancy look.

Grandma's Easy Butter Cookies

1 c. flour
1/2 c. butter, not margarine
4 Tbsp. brown sugar
1/2 c. chopped walnuts
Powdered sugar for dusting

Preheat oven to 350 degrees. Mix together flour, butter, brown sugar, and walnuts. Press into a 9"x9" pan. Bake until light brown. Cut into squares and dust with powdered sugar.

Hot Cider

2 quarts apple cider or juice
4 c. cranberry juice (not cranberry juice cocktail)
2 c. orange juice
2-3 cinnamon sticks
1 tsp. whole cloves
1/2 Tbsp. whole allspice
Brown sugar to taste

Combine all ingredients in saucepan and simmer. Strain when ready to serve.

Knobby Apple Cake

2 c. sugar
1 c. cooking oil
2 eggs
2 c. flour
2 tsp. cinnamon
1 tsp. nutmeg
1 tsp. salt
1 tsp. vanilla
4 c. apple chunks, peeled
1 c. chopped nuts
2 tsp. baking soda

Preheat oven to 350 degrees. Prepare a 9x13 baking dish with cooking spray. Cream together sugar and cooking oil. Add in eggs. Next add flour, cinnamon, nutmeg, salt, and vanilla. Finally, fold in apple chunks and nuts. Pour into 9x13 pan and bake for 40-60 minutes.

Mini Dessert Pizzas

1 roll of store bought sugar cookie dough
1 – 8 oz. container cream cheese, room
    temperature
Assortment of fresh fruit – strawberries,
blueberries, kiwi, mandarin orange, etc.

Cut dough into circles and bake as directed.
Allow to cool completely. Frost with cream
cheese and top with an assortment of fresh
sliced fruits.

Moist Coconut Cake

1 yellow cake mix
1 – 3.4 oz. pkg. instant vanilla pudding mix
1 can cream of coconut (example: Cocoa
    Lopez)
1 can sweetened condensed milk
1 – 8 oz. container whipped dessert topping
1 c. shredded coconut

Prepare cake as directed on box adding
in vanilla pudding mix. Bake in 9x13 pan.
When cake is done, poke holes all over cake
with fork.

Combine cream of coconut and sweetened
condensed milk. Mix well. Pour over cake
while still warm. Let cool. Frost with whipped
dessert topping and sprinkle with coconut.

Party Punch

2 large cans of pineapple juice
1 quart orange sherbet
1 quart vanilla ice cream
1 quart ginger ale

Combine pineapple juice, orange sherbet, and
vanilla ice cream. Beat well. Pour in ginger
ale and combine.

Poppy Seed Bundt Cake

1 yellow cake mix
1 – 3.4 oz. pkg. instant vanilla pudding mix
3 Tbsp. poppy seeds
1 c. water
1/2 c. vegetable oil
4 eggs
2 tsp. almond extract

Preheat oven to 350 degrees. Grease and
flour a 9-10 inch Bundt cake pan.

In a large bowl, combine cake mix, pudding
mix, and poppy seeds. Beat in water, oil,
and eggs on low until blended. Scrape sides
of the bowl and beat 4 minutes on medium
speed. Pour batter into prepared pan. Bake
for 50 minutes or until a toothpick inserted
into the center of the cake comes out clean.
Let cool in pan for 10 minutes, then turn out
onto wire rack to cool completely.

Sparkling Punch

2 quarts cranberry juice
1 – 6 oz. can pink lemonade concentrate,
    thawed
1 quart of sparkling water or lemon-lime soda

Combine all ingredients and chill. Makes 25
- 1/2 cup servings.

Optional garnish: freeze lemon slices and
strawberries or cherries in a gelatin mold ring
to float in punch bowl

Stove Top Chocolate Cookies

2 c. sugar
1/4 lb. butter or margarine
6 Tbsp. cocoa
1/2 c. milk
1/3 c. peanut butter
1 tsp. vanilla
3 c. quick-cooking oatmeal

Combine sugar, butter, cocoa, and milk in saucepan. Boil for 1 minute. Reduce heat and add peanut butter, vanilla, and oatmeal. Drop by spoonful onto wax paper and let cool completely.

Strawberry Pretzel Salad

1 1/2 c. crushed pretzels
4 1/2 Tbsp. sugar
3/4 c. butter, melted
1 c. sugar
2 – 8 oz. pkgs. cream cheese, softened
1 – 8 oz. container whipped dessert topping, thawed
1 – 6 oz. pkg. strawberry gelatin
2 c. boiling water
1 – 16 oz. pkg. frozen strawberries

Preheat oven to 350 degrees. Combine pretzels, sugar, and butter. Press into 9x13 pan and bake for 10 minutes. Cool completely.

Beat sugar and cream cheese together. Gently fold in whipped dessert topping. Spread over cooled pretzel crust. Refrigerate for at least 30 minutes.

Stir gelatin into boiling water. Mix in strawberries and stir until thawed. Cool slightly and pour over cream cheese mixture. Refrigerate for at least 1 hour.

Thanksgiving Day Punch

Orange Juice without pulp
Ginger Ale
Cranberry Juice (freeze some for ice cubes)

Combine equal parts of each juice and serve with cranberry cubes and optional orange slices.

Toffee Squares

1 c. butter
1 c. light brown sugar
1 egg yolk
1 tsp. vanilla
2 c. flour
1/4 tsp. salt
8 oz. chocolate chips
1 c. chopped nuts

Preheat oven to 350 degrees. Prepare 10x15" jelly roll pan with cooking spray.

Cream together butter and brown sugar. Add in egg yolk and vanilla. Blend in flour and salt and spread into jelly roll pan.

Bake for 20 minutes. Immediately after removing from oven, sprinkle with chocolate chips. After chips have started to melt, spread them like an icing all over the pan. Sprinkle with chopped nuts and cut into squares once cooled completely.

For this book

www.EntertainingForEternity.com
   Download invitations, buy additional books, contact Nan for speaking engagements, and more!

entertainingforeternity.blogspot.com
   Nan's blog where she posts current ideas and you can ask questions about the events you are planning.

Food Menus

Dinner preparation companies: These are where you go in to a central kitchen and prepare for a fee several meals at a time to take home and serve as you wish. It's a great way to learn how to cook new recipes and be ready for a busy week ahead or a dinner party. The sites below may not have an outlet in your area but check the web for your town.

www.savingdinner.com
   Includes weekly meal planning and shopping lists

www.letsdish.com

www.passyourplate.com

Recipes

The easiest thing to do is to type into your search engine "recipes for _____" filling the blank space with the food items you have on hand. Your search engine will give you many recipes to choose from all sorts of sites. For example: "recipe for leftover turkey" or "recipe for ground beef, tomatoes, green peppers, onions" List whatever ingredients you may have in your kitchen that need to be used up that night!

www.foodnetwork.com
   My favorite site! It has party ideas for any kind of party you could have with great recipes! I could spend a lot of time checking all this out!

www.allrecipes.com
   I use this all the time for my family. Lots of great recipes that are rated and also you can look up by ingredients etc.

www.cookinglight.com/cooking
   Cooking Light is a great magazine, too!

www.epicurious.com

www.bigoven.com
   My daughter's favorite site

www.teaforallreasons.com
   Recipes, tea, accessories and ideas for tea parties.

Grocery stores

Search the web for your local stores-these are in the North East USA:

www.safeway.com

www.giantfood.com/home
   See the "Easy Entertaining" section on this site!

People & Publications

Fabulous sites, full of ideas!
www.rachaelraymag.com
www.marthastewart.com
www.realsimple.com
www.countryhome.com
www.dominomag.com

Invitations & Stationary

www.123print.com
   Great place to buy everything from postcards and note cards to formal invitations.

www.evites.com
   Internet email invitations

Decorations & Supplies

www.homemadesimple.com
For great articles and ideas about simplifying everything from organization to decorations.

www.flylady.com
Before you start, get your home organized!

www.orientaltrading.com
Awesome site for party favors, decorations, and supplies. Year round ideas, even has Christian merchandise, inexpensive and affordable.

www.mninternational.com
It's full of things to order for entertaining decorations and supplies etc.

www.HolidayHistoryBrochures.com
These are excellent colorful handouts for your event as well as being a resource for developing an evangelistic talk around many different types of holidays.

Ministry Helps for Entertaining

www.christmasgatherings.org

www.familylifetoday.com

www.cefonline.com
Ideas for children's parties

www.jesusforchildren.org
Go to the Celebrate Jesus home parties section to download a complete manual I wrote for them with everything from games, coloring pages, invitations and exactly what to do for anytime of year.

www.leaderU.com
Has up to date articles about current issues.

www.apologetics.com
Answers the 20 toughest questions in defense of your faith.

www.campuscrusade.com/Tracts_and_Booklets/wouldpp.htm
Where to buy "How to Know God Personally" booklets

www.NewLifeResources.com
A great place to find and buy ministry materials.

www.petermarshallministries.com
To purchase The Light and the Glory by Peter Marshall.

Acknowledgements

Throughout the Word of God we are admonished to encourage fellow believers along the way. Encouragement is also a vital part of showing heavenly hospitality. This book would not have come into being without the encouragement of friends who have cheered me on, lent a helping hand or prayed for it. It's hard to remember and acknowledge everyone but here is a try at thanking so many dear friends.

Editors:
Beverly Hatfield Bowman
Flemming Saunders
Jana Spencer
Claudia Dunn

Graphic Artist:
Rebecca Blocher

Photographers:
Rebecca Blocher
Nancy Deliso
Nan McCullough

Inspirational Pioneers in Evangelistic Entertaining:
Art & Nancy DeMoss

Cheer Leaders and Prayer Warriors:
Jeannie Blocher, Carol Biedenharn, Vonette Bright, Art Dunn, Sarah Ellis, Dana Franklin, Amanda Henderson, Yvonne Lingo, Gail MacDonald, Will McGee, Ann Schwab, Mary Ward, Anne Marie Wenz, my Hospitality Task Force, my Women's Bible Study Group...
...and last and by no means least, my darling, helpful, patient husband Sam

Meet the Author

Nan McCullough is a woman of many and varied interests, having done just about everything from teaching Physical Education or coaching soccer to putting on elegant Teas. She is a mother, grandmother, ministry leader, evangelist, and inspiring speaker. Mostly, though, Nan is an enthusiastic and welcoming woman.

Since her three grown children have left the nest, her time is mostly spent in ministry activities. Nan worked with college students until she and her husband moved to the Washington, D.C. area to work with the Christian Embassy, a ministry of Campus Crusade for Christ. During her time there she led the Congressional Wives' Bible Study and now enjoys a ministry of evangelism and discipleship with women leaders. She is currently their "Women's Speaker at Large", speaking to wives of governors, congressmen, ambassadors, generals and admirals.

Additionally Nan has enjoyed leading women's groups in her church and neighborhood Bible studies including secular organizations like Capitol Speakers, Welcome to Washington and the Salvation Army Women's Auxiliary Board. She has enjoyed mentoring young women with the Titus 2 Ministry and speaking to MOPs (Mothers of Pre-schoolers) groups. Also, as Director of Evangelism for Body & Soul Fitness, she has trained and equipped others to share their faith and tell their stories.

Nan and her husband Sam have spent their lives extending hospitality and the Good News. They simply love having people in their home and nothing thrills Nan more than seeing someone come to a personal faith in Christ. One of the wonderful things about Nan is that she honestly has lived and used every bit of advice she put into this book for you.

She is the author of the manual, Heavenly Hospitality, which can be purchased from her website. It was the inspiration that led to her writing this book, Entertaining for Eternity. She also wrote a manual for The Jesus Film Project called Celebrate Jesus - Home Parties for Children, which can be purchased at www.jesusforchildren.org or by calling 800-432-1997.

Contact Nan directly at NanMcCullough@gmail.com or through her blog at entertainingforeternity.blogspot.com if you have questions or would like to have her come speak at an event. She would love to hear from you!